THE KITCHEN LIBRARY

HOME
BAKING

GW00361165

THE KITCHEN LIBRARY

HOME
BAKING

Carole Handslip

HAMLYN

CONTENTS

This edition published in 1990 by
The Hamlyn Publishing Group Limited,
a division of the Octopus Publishing Group,
Michelin House, 81 Fulham Road,
London SW3 6RB

© Cathay Books 1980

ISBN 0 600 56935 7

Produced by Mandarin Offset
Printed and Bound in Hong Kong

INTRODUCTION

There is nothing quite so appetizing as the warm aroma of freshly baked bread and cakes. Home baking is not the difficult, time-consuming task it is often assumed to be, and the results are most rewarding. With a few well-planned hours in the kitchen, you can produce a delicious variety of tea-time goodies.

For most bread, cake and biscuit making you will need very little equipment. A set of round cake tins, two square ones, a set of sandwich tins and a couple of loaf tins will be sufficient for most of the recipes in this book. For gâteaux, a French *moule a manqué* tin is ideal, as it produces a cake with sloping sides which allows the icing to spread evenly.

Pâtisserie is one area of baking that requires a certain amount of skill; but with practise and attention to detail, it is not difficult to achieve a professional result.

Whether you are experienced at baking or a beginner, the recipes in this book will prove enjoyable to make and the results – delicious!

NOTES

Standard spoon measurements are used in all recipes
1 tablespoon = one 15 ml spoon
1 teaspoon = one 5 ml spoon
All spoon measures are level.

If fresh yeast is unobtainable, substitute dried yeast but use only half the recommended quantity and follow the manufacturer's instructions for reconstituting.

Ovens should be preheated to the specified temperature.

For all recipes, quantities are given in both metric and imperial measures. Follow either set but not a mixture of both, because they are not interchangeable.

FAMILY CAKES & SPONGES

Chocolate Cake

200 g (7 oz) plain
   flour
1 teaspoon
   bicarbonate of soda
1 teaspoon baking
   powder
2 tablespoons cocoa
150 g (5 oz) soft
   brown sugar
2 tablespoons golden
   syrup
2 eggs
150 ml (¼ pint) oil
150 ml (¼ pint)
   milk

CHOCOLATE ICING:
175 g (6 oz) plain
   chocolate
2 tablespoons single
   cream

TO DECORATE:
walnut halves
icing sugar

Sift the dry ingredients into a mixing
bowl and make a well in the centre.
Add the syrup, eggs, oil and milk
and beat thoroughly until smooth.
Pour into a lined and greased 23 cm
(9 inch) cake tin and bake in a
preheated moderate oven, 160°C
(325°F), Gas Mark 3, for 45 to 50
minutes.

Leave in the tin for a few minutes
then turn onto a wire rack to cool.

To make the icing, place the
chocolate and cream in a small pan
and heat gently until melted. Cool
slightly, then pour over the cake.
Dredge the walnuts with icing sugar
and arrange around the top of the
cake.

Makes one 23 cm (9 inch) cake

Ginger Cake

175 g (6 oz) butter
or margarine
175 g (6 oz) caster
sugar
3 eggs
250 g (8 oz)
self-raising flour
½ teaspoon ground
ginger
75 g (3 oz)
preserved ginger,
chopped
2 tablespoons ginger
syrup
GINGER ICING:
175 g (6 oz) icing
sugar, sifted
2 tablespoons ginger
syrup
TO DECORATE:
preserved ginger
slices

Cream the fat and sugar together
until light and fluffy. Add the eggs
one at a time, adding a tablespoon of
flour with the last two. Sift and fold
in the remaining flour and the
ginger, then fold in the preserved
ginger and syrup. Turn into a lined
and greased 18 cm (7 inch) cake tin.

Bake in a preheated moderate
oven, 180°C (350°F), Gas Mark 4, for
1 to 1¼ hours. Turn onto a wire rack
to cool.

Beat the icing sugar and syrup
together until smooth. Pour over the
cake and leave until set. Decorate
with ginger slices.

Makes one 18 cm (7 inch) cake

Victoria Sandwich Cake

125 g (4 oz) butter
  or margarine
125 g (4 oz) caster
  sugar
2 eggs
125 g (4 oz)
  self-raising flour,
  sifted
1 tablespoon hot
  water

TO FINISH:
3 tablespoons jam
caster sugar

Line and grease two 18 cm (7 inch) sandwich tins.

Cream the fat and sugar together until light and fluffy. Beat in the eggs one at a time, adding a tablespoon of the flour with the second egg. Fold in the remaining flour, then the hot water.

Divide the mixture between the prepared tins and bake in a preheated moderate oven, 180°C (350°F), Gas Mark 4, for 20 to 25 minutes, until the cakes are golden and spring back when lightly pressed. Turn onto a wire rack to cool.

Sandwich the cakes together with the jam and sprinkle the top with caster sugar.

Makes one 18 cm (7 inch) cake

Angel Cake

25 g (1 oz) plain
 flour
25 g (1 oz) cornflour
150 g (5 oz) caster
 sugar
5 large egg whites
1 teaspoon vanilla
 essence
icing sugar for
 dredging

Sift the flours and 25 g (1 oz) of the caster sugar together 3 or 4 times.

Whisk the egg whites until stiff, add the remaining caster sugar a tablespoon at a time and continue whisking until very thick.

Carefully fold in the sifted mixture with the vanilla essence and turn into a 20 cm (8 inch) angel cake tin. Smooth the surface and bake in a preheated moderate oven, 180°C (350°F), Gas Mark 4, for 35 to 40 minutes, until the cake springs back when lightly pressed.

Turn it upside down on a wire rack and leave in the tin until cold, when the cake will fall easily from the tin. Serve sprinkled with icing sugar.

Makes one 20 cm (8 inch) angel cake

Apple and Cinnamon Cake

300 g (10 oz)
 self-raising flour
1 ½ teaspoons ground
 cinnamon
½ teaspoon salt
250 g (8 oz)
 demerara sugar
50 g (2 oz) raisins
125 g (4 oz) butter,
 melted
2 large eggs, beaten
175 ml (6 fl oz)
 milk
250 g (8 oz) apples,
 peeled, cored and
 chopped
icing sugar for
 dredging

Sift the flour, cinnamon and salt into a bowl and stir in the sugar and raisins. Mix in the melted butter, eggs, milk and apples and beat until smooth.

Turn into a lined and greased 20 cm (8 inch) square cake tin. Bake in a preheated moderate oven, 180°C (350°F), Gas Mark 4, for 1 to 1¼ hours until the cake springs back when lightly pressed.

Turn onto a wire rack to cool, then sprinkle with icing sugar.
Makes one 20 cm (8 inch) cake

Banana Cake

125 g (4 oz) butter
or margarine
125 g (4 oz) caster
sugar
2 eggs
125 g (4 oz)
self-raising flour,
sifted
2 bananas, mashed
FILLING:
50 g (2 oz) ground
almonds
50 g (2 oz) icing
sugar, sifted
1 small banana,
mashed
½ teaspoon lemon
juice
TO FINISH:
icing sugar

Cream the fat and sugar together until light and fluffy. Add the eggs one at a time, adding a tablespoon of flour with the second egg. Fold in the remaining flour with the bananas.

Divide the mixture between two 18 cm (7 inch) lined and greased sandwich tins. Bake in a preheated moderate oven, 180°C (350°F), Gas Mark 4, for 20 to 25 minutes until the cakes spring back when lightly pressed. Turn onto a wire rack to cool.

To make the filling, mix the ground almonds with the icing sugar, then add the banana and lemon juice and mix to a smooth paste. Sandwich the cakes together with the filling and dredge with icing sugar.

Makes one 18 cm (7 inch) cake

Genoese Sponge

50 g (2 oz) butter
4 eggs
125 g (4 oz) caster
  sugar
125 g (4 oz) plain
  flour, sifted
TO FINISH:
150 ml (5 fl oz)
  double cream
2 tablespoons lemon
  curd
icing sugar

Warm the butter gently until just soft – do not allow to become oily. Whisk the eggs and sugar in a mixing bowl over a pan of hot water until thick enough to leave a trail. Remove from the heat and whisk until cool. (Hot water is unnecessary if using an electric beater.)

Fold in the flour; when almost incorporated, fold in the butter as rapidly as possible, being careful not to knock out the air. Turn at once into a lined and greased 23 cm (9 inch) moule a manqué tin.

Bake in a preheated moderately hot oven, 190°C (375°F), Gas Mark 5, for 30 to 35 minutes until the cake springs back when lightly pressed. Leave in the tin for 1 minute then turn onto a wire rack to cool.

Whip the cream until stiff then whisk in the lemon curd. Split the cake in half and sandwich together with the lemon cream. Sprinkle with icing sugar.

Makes one 23 cm (9 inch) cake

Whisked Sponge

3 eggs
140 g (4½ oz) caster
  sugar
75 g (3 oz) plain
  flour, sifted
TO FINISH:
150 ml (¼ pint)
  double cream,
  whipped
2 tablespoons
  strawberry jam
icing sugar

Line, grease and flour a 23 cm (9 inch) moule a manqué tin.

Whisk the eggs and sugar in a mixing bowl over a pan of boiling water until thick enough to leave a trail. (Hot water is unnecessary if using an electric beater.)

Fold in the flour, then pour into the prepared tin. Bake in a preheated moderately hot oven, 190°C (375°F), Gas Mark 5, for 35 to 40 minutes until the cake springs back when lightly pressed.

Turn onto a wire rack to cool. Split the cake in half, then sandwich together with the cream and jam. Sprinkle with icing sugar.

Makes one 23 cm (9 inch) cake

Swiss Roll

3 eggs
125 g (4 oz) caster
 sugar
75 g (3 oz) plain
 flour, sifted
1 tablespoon hot
 water
3 tablespoons
 warmed jam
caster sugar for
 dredging

Line and grease an 18 x 28 cm (7 x 11 inch) Swiss roll tin.

Whisk eggs and sugar in a mixing bowl over a pan of hot water until thick enough to leave a trail. (Hot water is unnecessary if using an electric beater.) Fold in flour and water, then turn into prepared tin.

Bake in a preheated moderately hot oven, 200°C (400°F), Gas Mark 6, for 8 to 10 minutes until the cake springs back when lightly pressed.

Turn onto sugared greaseproof paper, peel off the lining paper and trim the edges. Cut two-thirds of the way through the short edge nearest you, then spread lightly with the jam and roll up quickly. Hold in position for a few minutes, then transfer to a wire rack to cool. Dredge with caster sugar before serving.

Makes one Swiss roll

Cherry Cake

175 g (6 oz) butter
  or margarine
175 g (6 oz) caster
  sugar
3 eggs
300 g (10 oz)
  self-raising flour,
  sifted
250 g (8 oz) glacé
  cherries, halved
50 g (2 oz) ground
  almonds
5 tablespoons milk
  (approximately)

Line and grease a deep 18 cm (7 inch) cake tin.

Cream the fat and sugar together until light and fluffy. Beat in the eggs one at a time, adding a tablespoon of flour with the last two.

Carefully fold in the remaining flour, then fold in the cherries, almonds and enough milk to give a dropping consistency.

Place in the prepared tin and bake in a preheated moderate oven, 160°C (325°F), Gas Mark 3, for 1½ to 2 hours.

Leave in the tin for 5 minutes, then turn onto a wire rack to cool.

Makes one 18 cm (7 inch) cake

Madeira Cake

250 g (8 oz) plain
  flour
1 teaspoon baking
  powder
175 g (6 oz) butter
  or margarine
175 g (6 oz) caster
  sugar
grated rind of ½
  lemon
3 eggs
2 tablespoons milk
2-3 strips citron peel

Line and grease a deep 18 cm (7 inch) cake tin. Sift the flour and baking powder together and set aside.

Cream the fat and sugar together with the lemon rind until light and fluffy. Beat in the eggs one at a time, adding a tablespoon of flour with the last two. Carefully fold in the remaining flour, then add the milk.

Place the mixture in the prepared tin and bake in a preheated moderate oven, 180°C (350°F), Gas Mark 4, for 1 hour. Arrange the citron peel on top of the cake and bake for a further 30 minutes.

Leave in the tin for 5 minutes, then turn onto a wire rack to cool.
Makes one 18 cm (7 inch) cake

Marmalade Cake

250 g (8 oz)
  self-raising flour
1 teaspoon ground
  mixed spice
175 g (6 oz) butter
  or margarine
175 g (6 oz) soft
  brown sugar
grated rind and juice
  of 1 orange
3 eggs
2 tablespoons thick
  marmalade
75 g (3 oz) mixed
  dried fruit
2 tablespoons milk
ORANGE ICING:
175 g (6 oz) icing
  sugar, sifted
grated rind and juice
  of ½ orange
TO DECORATE:
thinly pared rind of
  ½ orange,
  shredded

Line and grease an 18 cm (7 inch) cake tin. Sift the flour and spice together and set aside.

Cream the butter or margarine, sugar and orange rind together until light and fluffy. Beat in the eggs one at a time, adding a tablespoon of flour with the last two. Fold in the marmalade, then fold in the remaining flour with the mixed fruit, orange juice and milk.

Turn into the prepared tin and bake in a preheated moderate oven, 180°C (350°F), Gas Mark 4, for 1¼ to 1½ hours. Leave in the tin for a few minutes, then turn onto a wire rack to cool.

Place the icing ingredients in a bowl and beat until smooth. Pour over the top of the cake; leave until set. Blanch the shredded rind in boiling water, drain thoroughly, then use to decorate the cake.
Makes one 18 cm (7 inch) cake

Dundee Cake

175 g (6 oz) plain
  flour
1 teaspoon ground
  mixed spice
125 g (4 oz) butter
  or margarine
125 g (4 oz) soft
  brown sugar
grated rind of
  ½ orange or
  lemon
3 eggs
125 g (4 oz)
  sultanas
125 g (4 oz) currants
125 g (4 oz) raisins
50 g (2 oz) glacé
  cherries, quartered
25 g (1 oz) chopped
  mixed peel
40 g (1½ oz) split
  blanched almonds
  to decorate

Prepare a deep 15 cm (6 inch) cake tin as for Boiled Fruit Cake (see opposite).

Sift the flour and spice together. Cream the fat, sugar and orange rind together until light and fluffy. Beat in the eggs one at a time, adding a tablespoon of flour with the last two. Fold in the remaining flour and the fruit until thoroughly mixed.

Place in the prepared tin, smooth the top and decorate with the almonds. Bake in a preheated moderate oven, 160°C (325°F), Gas Mark 3, for 1 hour, then lower the temperature to 150°C (300°F), Gas Mark 2, and bake for a further 2 to 2½ hours or until a skewer inserted into the centre comes out clean.

Leave in the tin for 5 minutes then turn onto a wire rack to cool.
Makes one 15 cm (6 inch) cake

Farmhouse Fruit Cake

250 g (8 oz)
  self-raising flour
1 teaspoon ground
  mixed spice
150 g (5 oz) butter
  or margarine
150 g (5 oz) soft
  brown sugar
1 tablespoon black
  treacle
2 eggs
125 g (4 oz) dates,
  stoned and
  chopped
125 g (4 oz)
  sultanas
125 g (4 oz) currants
25 g (1 oz) chopped
  mixed peel
3 tablespoons milk

Prepare a deep 18 cm (7 inch) square cake tin as for Boiled Fruit Cake (see opposite). Sift the flour and spice together and set aside.

Cream the butter or margarine, sugar and treacle together until light and fluffy. Beat in the eggs one at a time, adding a tablespoon of flour with the second egg. Fold in the remaining flour with the fruit and milk; mix thoroughly.

Turn into the prepared tin and bake in a preheated moderate oven, 160°C (325°F), Gas Mark 3, for 2 to 2½ hours, or until a skewer inserted into the centre comes out clean.

Leave in the tin for 5 minutes then turn onto a wire rack to cool.
Makes one 18 cm (7 inch) cake

Boiled Fruit Cake

150 g (5 oz) butter
or margarine
175 g (6 oz) golden
syrup
175 ml (6 fl oz)
milk
250 g (8 oz) currants
125 g (4 oz)
sultanas
125 g (4 oz) dates,
chopped
125 g (4 oz) raisins
50 g (2 oz) chopped
mixed peel
250 g (8 oz) plain
flour
2 teaspoons ground
mixed spice
1/2 teaspoon
bicarbonate of soda
2 eggs, beaten

Grease a deep 18 cm (7 inch) cake tin and line the base and sides with a double layer of greased greaseproof paper. Tie a thick band of brown paper around the outside of the tin and stand it on a pad of brown paper on a baking sheet.

Put the fat, syrup, milk and fruit in a pan and heat slowly until the fat has melted. Simmer gently for 5 minutes, stirring occasionally, then remove from the heat and cool.

Sift the flour, spice and soda into a bowl, add the syrup mixture and the eggs and beat together thoroughly.

Place in the prepared tin and bake in a preheated cool oven, 150°C (300°F), Gas Mark 2, for 2 to 2¼ hours, or until a skewer inserted into the centre comes out clean. Leave in the tin for 5 minutes, then turn onto a wire rack to cool.

Makes one 18 cm (7 inch) cake

Devil's Food Cake

50 g (2 oz) cocoa
200 ml (⅓ pint)
    boiling water
175 g (6 oz) plain
    flour
¼ teaspoon baking
    powder
1 teaspoon
    bicarbonate of soda
125 g (4 oz) butter
    or margarine
300 g (10 oz) caster
    sugar
2 eggs, beaten
BUTTER ICING:
1 tablespoon cocoa
1 tablespoon hot
    water
50 g (2 oz) butter or
    margarine
125 g (4 oz) icing
    sugar, sifted
FUDGE ICING:
50 g (2 oz) butter or
    margarine
2 tablespoons milk
2 tablespoons cocoa
250 g (8 oz) icing
    sugar, sifted
TO DECORATE:
8 walnut halves

Line and grease two 20 cm (8 inch) sandwich tins.

Blend the cocoa with half the water until smooth. Stir in the remaining water and leave to cool. Sift the flour, baking powder and soda together.

Cream the fat and sugar and 3 tablespoons of the cocoa mixture together until light and fluffy. Gradually beat in the eggs.

Fold in the flour alternately with the remaining cocoa. The mixture may curdle at this stage but will not affect the result.

Divide the mixture between the prepared cake tins and bake in a preheated moderate oven, 180°C (350°F), Gas Mark 4, for 45 to 50 minutes until firm to the touch. Leave in the tins for 5 minutes, then turn onto a wire rack to cool.

To make the butter icing, blend the cocoa with the hot water, then leave to cool. Beat the butter or margarine with half the icing sugar until light and fluffy. Add the cocoa mixture and remaining icing sugar and beat until smooth. Sandwich the cake layers together with the butter icing.

To make the fudge icing, place the butter or margarine, milk and cocoa in a pan and heat gently until melted. Cool slightly, then add the icing sugar and beat until smooth. Spread over the top and sides of the cake. Decorate with the walnut halves.
Makes one 20 cm (8 inch) cake

Chocolate Almond Cake

125 g (4 oz) plain
  chocolate
125 g (4 oz) butter
  or margarine
125 g (4 oz) caster
  sugar
4 eggs, separated
125 g (4 oz) ground
  almonds
50 g (2 oz) plain
  flour, sifted
ICING:
175 g (6 oz) plain
  chocolate
1 tablespoon water
25 g (1 oz) butter

Melt the chocolate in a basin over a
pan of hot water. Cream the fat and
sugar together until light and fluffy,
then beat in the chocolate. Beat the
egg yolks into the creamed mixture,
then beat in the almonds and flour.

Whisk the egg whites until stiff
and carefully fold into the cake
mixture. Pour into a lined and
greased 18 cm (7 inch) square cake
tin and bake in a preheated moderate
oven, 160°C (325°F), Gas Mark 3, for
50 minutes to 1 hour. Leave in the tin
for 5 minutes, then cool on a wire rack.

Beat the icing ingredients in a
basin over a pan of hot water. Cool
slightly, then spread three-quarters of
the icing over the cake; leave to set.
Place the remaining icing in a small
piping bag fitted with a writing
nozzle and pipe lines over the top.
Makes one 18 cm (7 inch) cake

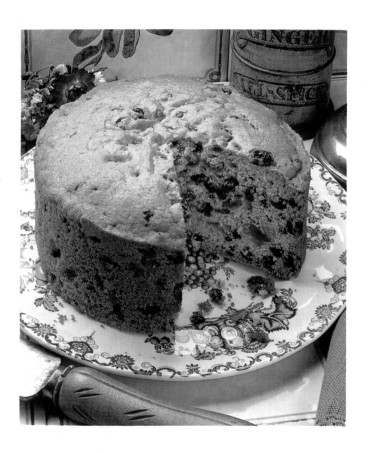

Everyday Fruit Cake

250 g (8 oz)
    self-raising flour
½ teaspoon ground
    mixed spice
½ teaspoon ground
    cinnamon
125 g (4 oz) butter
    or margarine
125 g (4 oz) soft
    brown sugar
125 g (4 oz)
    sultanas
125 g (4 oz) currants
50 g (2 oz) glacé
    cherries, quartered
1 large egg
5 tablespoons milk

Line and grease a deep 15 cm (6 inch)
cake tin. Sift the flour and spices into
a mixing bowl, add the fat and rub in
until the mixture resembles
breadcrumbs. Stir in the sugar and
fruit. Whisk the egg and milk
together, add to the mixture and beat
thoroughly.

Place in the prepared tin and bake
in a preheated moderate oven, 180°C
(350°F), Gas Mark 4, for 1¼ to 1½
hours. Leave in the tin for a few
minutes, then turn onto a wire rack
to cool.

Makes one 15 cm (6 inch) cake

Crystallized Fruit Cake

175 g (6 oz) butter
or margarine
175 g (6 oz) soft
brown sugar
250 g (8 oz) plain
flour
1 teaspoon ground
mixed spice
3 eggs
250 g (8 oz) raisins
125 g (4 oz)
sultanas
25 g (1 oz) angelica
125 g (4 oz) glacé
cherries, quartered
25 g (1 oz)
crystallized ginger
1 tablespoon sherry
TO DECORATE:
75 g (3 oz)
crystallized fruits
50 g (2 oz) walnuts
APRICOT GLAZE:
2 tablespoons apricot
jam
1 tablespoon water
squeeze of lemon
juice

Prepare a deep 18 cm (7 inch) cake tin as for Boiled Fruit Cake (page 17).

Cream the fat and sugar together until light and fluffy. Sift the flour with the mixed spice. Beat in the eggs one at a time, adding a tablespoon of flour with the last two. Fold in the remaining flour with the fruit, ginger and sherry.

Turn into the prepared tin and decorate with the crystallized fruits and walnuts. Bake in a preheated moderate oven, 160°C (325°F), Gas Mark 3, for 1 hour, then lower the temperature to 150°C (300°F), Gas Mark 2, and bake for a further 2 hours until a skewer inserted into the centre comes out clean. Leave in the tin for 5 minutes then turn onto a wire rack to cool.

For the apricot glaze, place the jam and water in a small pan and boil for 3 to 4 minutes. Stir in the lemon juice, then sieve, return to the pan and heat gently. Brush over the fruit.
Makes one 18 cm (7 inch) cake

Sticky Gingerbread

250 g (8 oz) plain
  flour
3 teaspoons ground
  ginger
1 teaspoon ground
  mixed spice
1 teaspoon
  bicarbonate of soda
125 g (4 oz) butter
  or margarine
75 g (3 oz) black
  treacle
125 g (4 oz) golden
  syrup
50 g (2 oz) soft
  brown sugar
150 ml (¼ pint)
  milk
2 eggs, beaten
25 g (1 oz) shredded
  almonds

Sift the flour, spices and soda into a
mixing bowl. Put the fat, treacle,
syrup and sugar in a pan and heat
gently. Cool slightly then add to the
dry ingredients with the milk and
eggs and mix thoroughly.

Pour into a lined and greased
18 cm (7 inch) square cake tin,
sprinkle with almonds, and bake in a
preheated moderate oven, 160°C
(325°F), Gas Mark 3, for 1½ to 2
hours or until a skewer inserted into
the centre comes out clean.

Leave in the tin for 15 minutes,
then turn onto a wire rack to cool.
Store in an airtight tin for several
days before eating.

Makes one 18 cm (7 inch) cake
NOTE: Replace the ground ginger
with finely chopped fresh root
ginger, if preferred.

Parkin

250 g (8 oz)
   wholewheat flour
250 g (8 oz) *rolled*
   oats
½ teaspoon
   bicarbonate of soda
½ teaspoon salt
1 teaspoon ground
   ginger
125 g (4 oz) *butter*
125 g (4 oz) *black*
   treacle
125 g (4 oz) *golden*
   syrup
125 g (4 oz) *soft*
   brown sugar
175 ml (6 fl oz)
   milk

Place the flour and oats in a mixing
bowl and sift in the soda, salt and
ginger. Place the butter, treacle,
syrup and sugar in a saucepan and
heat gently. Cool slightly, then add
to the dry ingredients, together with
the milk; mix thoroughly.

Pour into a lined and greased
20 cm (8 inch) square cake tin and
bake in a preheated moderate oven,
180°C (350°F), Gas Mark 4, for 50 to
60 minutes until the cake is firm to
the touch.

Leave in the tin for 15 minutes
then turn onto a wire rack to cool.
Store in an airtight tin for several
days before eating.

Makes one 20 cm (8 inch) cake

Macaroons

250 g (8 oz) caster
   sugar
150 g (5 oz) ground
   almonds
1 tablespoon rice
   flour
2 egg whites
rice paper
25 split almonds

Mix the sugar, almonds and rice flour together and set aside. Beat the egg whites lightly, add the dry ingredients, and beat to a smooth, firm consistency.

Leave to stand for 5 minutes then roll into small balls and place slightly apart on a baking sheet lined with rice paper. Flatten slightly and place a split almond on each one.

Bake in a preheated moderate oven, 180°C (350°F), Gas Mark 4, for 20 minutes. Cool on the baking sheet.

Makes 25

Almond Galettes

125 g (4 oz) butter
or margarine
50 g (2 oz) caster
sugar
1 egg yolk
50 g (2 oz) ground
almonds
175 g (6 oz) plain
flour
TOPPING:
125 g (4 oz) icing
sugar, sifted
1 egg white
50 g (2 oz) shredded
almonds

Cream the butter or margarine and sugar together, then add the egg yolk and beat well. Add the ground almonds and flour and mix well. Knead lightly and roll out thinly. Cut into rounds using a 6 cm (2½ inch) plain cutter and place on a greased baking sheet.

For the topping, mix the icing sugar with the egg white, then add the shredded almonds and stir well. Spoon over the biscuits and bake in a preheated moderate oven, 180°C (350°F), Gas Mark 4, for 15 to 20 minutes until golden brown. Cool on the baking sheet.

Makes 24

Oat Crunchies

125 g (4 oz) rolled
    oats
50 g (2 oz) medium
    oatmeal
150 g (5 oz) soft
    brown sugar
120 ml (4 fl oz)
    vegetable oil
1 egg
½ teaspoon almond
    essence

Place the oats, oatmeal, sugar and oil in a bowl, mix well and leave to stand for 1 hour. Add the egg and almond essence and beat together thoroughly. Place teaspoonfuls of the mixture well apart on a greased baking sheet and press flat with a damp fork.

Bake in a preheated moderate oven, 160°C (325°F), Gas Mark 3, for 15 to 20 minutes until golden brown. Leave to cool for 2 minutes then transfer to a wire rack to cool completely.
Makes 30

Flapjacks

125 g (4 oz)
  margarine
125 g (4 oz) soft
  brown sugar
75 g (3 oz) golden
  syrup
250 g (8 oz) rolled
  oats

Melt the margarine with the sugar
and syrup, then stir in the rolled oats
and mix thoroughly. Turn into a
greased shallow 20 cm (8 inch)
square tin, and smooth the top with
a palette knife.

Bake in a preheated moderate
oven, 180°C (350°F), Gas Mark 4, for
25 to 30 minutes until golden brown.

Cool in the tin for 2 minutes, then
cut into fingers. Cool completely
before removing from the tin.
Makes 16

Chocolate Chip Biscuits

125 g (4 oz) butter
  or margarine
50 g (2 oz) caster
  sugar
1 egg, beaten
150 g (5 oz)
  self-raising flour,
  sifted
175 g (6 oz) plain
  chocolate, chopped

Beat the butter or margarine and sugar together until light and fluffy. Add the egg and beat thoroughly. Fold in the flour and chocolate.

Place teaspoonfuls of the mixture a little apart on a greased baking sheet and bake in a preheated moderate oven, 180°C (350°F), Gas Mark 4, for 15 to 20 minutes. Transfer to a wire rack to cool.
Makes 25 to 30

Coconut Cookies

125 g (4 oz) butter
175 g (6 oz) sugar
1 egg, beaten
75 g (3 oz)
  desiccated coconut
175 g (6 oz)
  self-raising flour,
  sifted

Cream the butter until soft, then add the sugar and beat until light and fluffy. Add the egg and beat thoroughly. Add half the coconut and the flour and stir until mixed. Form into small balls and roll in the remaining coconut.

Place slightly apart on a greased baking sheet and flatten with a palette knife. Bake in a preheated moderately hot oven, 190°C (375°F), Gas Mark 5, for 10 to 15 minutes. Transfer to a wire rack to cool.
Makes 40

Cinnamon Crisps

125 g (4 oz)
  wholewheat flour
50 g (2 oz) rolled
  oats
75 g (3 oz) sugar
½ teaspoon
  bicarbonate of soda
1 teaspoon ground
  cinnamon
75 g (3 oz) butter or
  margarine
1 tablespoon golden
  syrup
1 tablespoon milk

Place the flour, oats and sugar in a bowl, sift in the soda and cinnamon and mix thoroughly. Place the butter or margarine, syrup and milk in a pan and heat until the fat has melted. Pour into the dry ingredients and beat until smooth.

Shape into small balls and place slightly apart on a greased baking sheet, flattening with a palette knife.

Bake in a preheated moderate oven, 180°C (350°F), Gas Mark 4, for 15 minutes until golden brown. Cool on the baking sheet.
Makes 25

Date and Oat Slices

175 g (6 oz)
   wholewheat flour
175 g (6 oz) rolled
   oats
175 g (6 oz) butter
   or margarine
50 g (2 oz) soft
   brown sugar
FILLING:
175 g (6 oz) dates,
   stoned and
   chopped
2 tablespoons water
1 tablespoon lemon
   juice
1 tablespoon clear
   honey

Place the filling ingredients in a small pan and simmer gently until the dates are soft.

Meanwhile, mix the flour and oats together, then rub in the butter or margarine. Stir in the sugar and place half the mixture in a lined and greased shallow 18 cm (7 inch) square tin, pressing down firmly. Cover with the date mixture, sprinkle over the remaining oat mixture and press down well.

Bake in a preheated moderately hot oven, 190°C (375°F), Gas Mark 5, for 35 to 40 minutes. Cut into slices while warm, then cool completely in the tin before removing carefully.
Makes 12

Digestive Biscuits

175 g (6 oz)
 wholewheat flour
25 g (1 oz) oatmeal
½ teaspoon salt
1 teaspoon baking
 powder
75 g (3 oz) butter or
 margarine
40 g (1½ oz) soft
 brown sugar
2-3 tablespoons milk

Mix the flour and oatmeal together, then sift in the salt and baking powder. Rub in the butter or margarine until the mixture resembles breadcrumbs, then stir in the sugar. Add the milk and mix to a stiff dough. Roll out thinly, prick well and cut into 6 cm (2½ inch) rounds with a plain cutter.

Place on a greased baking sheet and bake in a preheated moderately hot oven, 190°C (375°F), Gas Mark 5, for 15 to 20 minutes. Transfer to a wire rack to cool. Serve with cheese if liked.

Makes 22

Walnut Cookies

175 g (6 oz) plain
  flour
1 teaspoon baking
  powder
½ teaspoon
  bicarbonate of soda
75 g (3 oz) sugar
75 g (3 oz) butter or
  margarine
50 g (2 oz) walnuts,
  chopped
3 tablespoons golden
  syrup

Sift the flour, baking powder and
soda together in a bowl and add the
sugar. Rub in the fat until the
mixture resembles breadcrumbs,
then stir in the walnuts. Add the
syrup and mix by hand to a firm
dough. Form into balls about the size
of a walnut and place slightly apart
on a greased baking sheet.

Bake in a preheated moderately
hot oven, 190°C (375°F), Gas Mark
5, for 15 minutes until golden
brown. Transfer to a wire rack to
cool.

Makes 20

Brownies

125 g (4 oz)
   self-raising flour
¼ teaspoon baking
   powder
125 g (4 oz) plain
   chocolate
125 g (4 oz) butter
   or margarine
125 g (4 oz) soft
   brown sugar
2 eggs
75 g (3 oz) walnuts,
   chopped

Sift the flour and baking powder together and set aside. Melt the chocolate in a small bowl over a pan of hot water.

Cream the butter or margarine and sugar together until light and fluffy. Beat in the eggs one at a time, adding a tablespoon of flour with the second egg. Beat in the melted chocolate, then fold in the remaining flour and the walnuts.

Place in a greased and lined shallow 20 cm (8 inch) square tin and bake in a preheated moderate oven, 180°C (350°F), Gas Mark 4, for 30 to 35 minutes.

Cut into squares while still warm, then leave to cool in the tin.
Makes 16

Chocolate Crunch

50 g (2 oz) butter or
   margarine
50 g (2 oz) golden
   syrup
125 g (4 oz) plain
   chocolate
75 g (3 oz)
   cornflakes
25 g (1 oz)
   desiccated coconut

Place the butter or margarine, syrup and chocolate in a pan and stir over low heat until melted. Add the cornflakes and coconut and mix well. Turn into a lined and greased 20 cm (8 inch) sandwich tin and chill until set. Cut into wedges to serve.
Makes one 20 cm (8 inch) round

Coconut Pyramids

2 egg whites
150 g (5 oz) caster
   sugar
150 g (5 oz)
   desiccated coconut
1 teaspoon cornflour
red food colouring
rice paper

Whisk the egg whites until stiff, then fold in the sugar, coconut and cornflour. Divide the mixture in half and colour one half pink. Place small mounds of the mixture on a baking sheet lined with rice paper and shape into pyramids.

Bake in a preheated moderate oven, 180°C (350°F), Gas Mark 4, for 8 to 10 minutes until lightly browned.
Makes 12

Chocolate Caramel Fingers

125 g (4 oz) butter
50 g (2 oz) caster
   sugar
175 g (6 oz) plain
   flour, sifted
CARAMEL FILLING:
125 g (4 oz) butter
   or margarine
50 g (2 oz) caster
   sugar
2 tablespoons golden
   syrup
150 ml (5 fl oz)
   condensed milk
CHOCOLATE
   TOPPING:
125 g (4 oz) plain
   chocolate
15 g (½ oz) butter

Cream the butter and sugar together until light and fluffy. Add the flour and stir until the mixture binds together. Knead until smooth.

Roll out to a square and press evenly into a shallow 20 cm (8 inch) square tin and prick well. Bake in a preheated moderate oven, 180°C (350°F), Gas Mark 4, for 25 to 30 minutes. Cool in the tin.

Place the filling ingredients in a saucepan and stir until dissolved. Bring slowly to the boil, then cook, stirring, for 5 to 7 minutes. Cool slightly, then spread over the biscuit mixture and leave to set.

For the topping, melt the chocolate with the butter over low heat and spread over the caramel. Leave until set, then cut into fingers.
Makes 14

Chocolate Biscuit Cake

125 g (4 oz)
   margarine
50 g (2 oz) caster
   sugar
2 tablespoons golden
   syrup
2 tablespoons milk
2 tablespoons
   drinking chocolate
1 tablespoon cocoa
250 g (8 oz)
   digestive biscuits,
   crushed
50 g (2 oz) cake
   crumbs
50 g (2 oz) glacé
   cherries, chopped
50 g (2 oz) raisins
CHOCOLATE ICING:
125 g (4 oz) plain
   chocolate
15 g (½ oz) butter

Place the margarine, sugar, syrup and milk in a pan and heat gently. Add the drinking chocolate, cocoa and half the biscuits and mix well. Add the remaining ingredients and stir until thoroughly mixed, then press into a 20 cm (8 inch) sandwich tin. Chill in the refrigerator until set, then remove from the tin.

Melt the chocolate and butter in a small bowl over a pan of hot water and mix well. Spread over the biscuit mixture and allow to set, then cut into wedges.
Makes one 20 cm (8 inch) round

Ginger Nuts

50 g (2 oz) butter or
  margarine
4 tablespoons golden
  syrup
50 g (2 oz) soft
  brown sugar
175 g (6 oz)
  self-raising flour
1 teaspoon ground
  ginger

Melt the butter or margarine, syrup and sugar together in a saucepan. Cool, then sift in the flour and ginger and mix to a smooth paste. Roll into small balls the size of a walnut, place well apart on a greased baking sheet and flatten slightly.

Bake in a preheated moderately hot oven, 190°C (375°F), Gas Mark 5, for 15 to 20 minutes. Leave on the sheet for 1 minute, then transfer to a wire rack to cool.
Makes 25 to 30

Uncooked Chocolate Bars

50 g (2 oz) butter or
  margarine
200 g (7 oz) plain
  chocolate
3 tablespoons golden
  syrup
250 g (8 oz)
  digestive biscuits,
  crushed

Place the butter or margarine, chocolate and syrup in a saucepan and heat gently until melted. Stir in the biscuits and mix thoroughly.

Turn into a greased and lined shallow 18 cm (7 inch) square tin and smooth the top with a palette knife. Leave to set, then cut into bars.
Makes 16

Chocolate Crisps

125 g (4 oz) butter
  or margarine
50 g (2 oz) caster
  sugar
125 g (4 oz)
  self-raising flour
25 g (1 oz) cocoa

Beat the butter or margarine and sugar together until light and fluffy. Sift in the flour and cocoa and mix well. Form into small balls about the size of a walnut, place on a greased baking sheet and flatten with a damp fork. Bake in a preheated moderately hot oven, 190°C (375°F), Gas Mark 5, for 10 to 15 minutes. Transfer to a wire rack to cool.
Makes 24

Wholewheat Biscuits

75 g (3 oz)
  self-raising flour
½ teaspoon ground
  mixed spice
75 g (3 oz)
  wholewheat flour
25 g (1 oz) oatmeal
125 g (4 oz) butter
  or margarine
50 g (2 oz) demerara
  sugar
2 tablespoons milk

Sift the flour and spice into a bowl, then stir in the wholewheat flour and oatmeal. Rub in the fat until the mixture resembles breadcrumbs, add the sugar and mix to a firm dough with the milk.

Turn onto a floured surface, knead lightly then roll out very thinly. Cut into 7.5 cm (3 inch) rounds using a fluted cutter and place on a greased baking sheet. Bake in a preheated moderately hot oven, 190°C (375°F), Gas Mark 5, for 15 minutes. Transfer to a wire rack to cool.
Makes 18 to 20

Scones

250 g (8 oz) plain
  flour
1 teaspoon cream of
  tartar
1/2 teaspoon
  bicarbonate of soda
1/2 teaspoon salt
50 g (2 oz) butter or
  margarine
25 g (1 oz) caster
  sugar
120 ml (4 fl oz)
  milk
milk to glaze

Sift the flour, cream of tartar, soda and salt into a mixing bowl and rub in the butter or margarine until the mixture resembles breadcrumbs. Stir in the sugar, add the milk and mix to a soft dough.

Turn onto a floured surface, knead lightly and roll out to a 2 cm (3/4 inch) thickness. Cut into 5 cm (2 inch) rounds with a fluted cutter. Place on a floured baking sheet and brush with milk. Bake in a preheated hot oven, 220°C (425°F), Gas Mark 7, for 12 to 15 minutes. Transfer to a wire rack to cool. Serve with jam and butter or cream.

Makes 12 to 14

DATE SCONES: Sift 1/2 teaspoon ground cinnamon with the flour and mix in 50 g (2 oz) finely chopped dates with the sugar.

WHOLEWHEAT SCONES: Replace 125 g (4 oz) plain flour with 125 g (4 oz) wholewheat flour.

Fruit Scone Round

250 g (8 oz)
  self-raising flour
1 teaspoon baking
  powder
50 g (2 oz) butter or
  margarine
25 g (1 oz) caster
  sugar
75 g (3 oz) currants
  or sultanas
120 ml (4 fl oz)
  milk
milk to glaze

Sift the flour and baking powder into a bowl and rub in the fat until the mixture resembles breadcrumbs. Stir in the sugar and fruit, add the milk and mix to a soft dough.

Turn onto a floured surface, knead lightly then form into an 18 cm (7 inch) round and place on a floured baking sheet.

Score the round into 8 sections, brush with milk and bake in a preheated moderately hot oven, 200°C (400°F), Gas Mark 6, for 15 to 20 minutes until golden brown. Transfer to a wire rack to cool and serve with butter and jam.

Makes one 18 cm (7 inch) round

Cheese-Topped Scones

250 g (8 oz)
    self-raising flour
1 teaspoon mustard
pinch of cayenne
    pepper
½ teaspoon salt
50 g (2 oz) butter or
    margarine
125 g (4 oz) cheese,
    grated
1 egg, beaten
4 tablespoons milk
milk to glaze

Sift the flour, mustard, cayenne and salt into a bowl and rub in the fat until the mixture resembles breadcrumbs. Stir in 75 g (3 oz) of the cheese, the egg and milk and mix to a soft dough.

Turn onto a floured surface, knead lightly and roll out to a 2 cm (¾ inch) thickness. Cut into 5 cm (2 inch) rounds with a plain cutter and place on a floured baking sheet. Brush with milk and sprinkle with the remaining cheese.

Bake in a preheated moderately hot oven, 200°C (400°F), Gas Mark 6, for 15 to 20 minutes. Transfer to a wire rack to cool. Serve with butter.
Makes 10

Drop Scones

250 g (8 oz) plain
  flour
1 teaspoon cream of
  tartar
½ teaspoon
  bicarbonate of soda
½ teaspoon salt
25 g (1 oz) caster
  sugar
1 large egg
250 ml (8 fl oz)
  milk
1 tablespoon oil

Sift the dry ingredients together into a mixing bowl and make a well in the centre. Add the egg and half the milk and mix to a smooth batter. Gradually beat in the remaining milk with the oil, mixing to a thick batter.

Heat a heavy frying pan or griddle and grease lightly. Drop tablespoonfuls of the batter onto the griddle and cook until the top is blistered. Turn with a palette knife and cook until the underside is golden brown. Place the scones inside a clean folded tea-towel to keep moist until they are all cooked. Serve with butter.

Makes 12 to 16

40

Shortbread

125 g (4 oz) butter
50 g (2 oz) caster
  sugar
175 g (6 oz) plain
  flour, sifted
caster sugar for
  dredging

Cream the butter and sugar together until light and fluffy. Add the flour and stir until the mixture binds together.

Turn onto a lightly floured board and knead until smooth. Roll out to a 20 cm (8 inch) round and place on a greased baking sheet. Pinch the edges with your fingers, prick well with a fork and mark into 8 portions.

Dust with caster sugar and bake in a preheated moderate oven, 160°C (325°F), Gas Mark 3, for 40 to 45 minutes until pale golden. Leave on the baking sheet for 5 minutes, then transfer to a wire rack to cool completely.

Makes one 20 cm (8 inch) round

GÂTEAUX

Chocolate and Chestnut Gâteau

75 g (3 oz) plain
  chocolate
2 tablespoons water
4 eggs, separated
250 g (8 oz) caster
  sugar
350 g (12 oz)
  chestnuts, cooked
  and sieved

TO FINISH:
284 ml (10 fl oz)
  double cream,
  whipped
1 marron glacé

Melt the chocolate and water in a bowl over a pan of hot water. Add the egg yolks and sugar and whisk until thick enough to leave a trail. Whisk the egg whites until stiff, then fold into the mixture with the chestnuts.

Turn into two lined and greased 20 cm (8 inch) sandwich tins and bake in a preheated moderate oven, 180°C (350°F), Gas Mark 4, for 35 to 40 minutes. Leave for a few minutes, then turn onto a wire rack to cool.

Use half the cream to sandwich the cakes together. Spread 2 tablespoons cream over the top of the cake and pipe the remainder in rosettes to decorate. Place a piece of marron glacé on each rosette.

Makes one 20 cm (8 inch) gâteau

Gâteau Normande

WHISKED SPONGE:
3 eggs
140 g (4½ oz) caster sugar
75 g (3 oz) plain flour, sifted
1 teaspoon ground mixed spice
FILLING AND TOPPING:
500 g (1 lb) apples, peeled, cored and sliced
2 tablespoons apricot jam
50 g (2 oz) sultanas
50 g (2 oz) raisins
2 tablespoons soft brown sugar
284 ml (10 fl oz) double cream, whipped

Prepare and bake the sponge as for Whisked Sponge (page 12), adding the spice with the flour.

Place the apples and apricot jam in a pan, cover and cook over a gentle heat until soft. Stir in the dried fruit and sugar, then leave to cool.

Split the cake in half and sandwich together with the apple filling and one third of the cream.

Swirl another third of the cream over the top of the cake and pipe the remainder in rosettes around the edge.

Makes one 23 cm (9 inch) gâteau

Gâteau au Chocolat

3 eggs
140 g (4½ oz) caster sugar
50 g (2 oz) plain flour
25 g (1 oz) cocoa
CHOCOLATE CARAQUE:
75 g (3 oz) plain chocolate
BUTTER CREAM:
2 egg whites
125 g (4 oz) icing sugar
125 g (4 oz) unsalted butter
50 g (2 oz) plain chocolate, melted

Line and grease a 23 cm (9 inch) moule a manqué tin.

Place the eggs and sugar in a bowl and whisk over a pan of boiling water until thickened. (The hot water is unnecessary if using an electric beater.) Sift and fold in the flour and cocoa. Pour into the prepared tin and bake in a preheated moderately hot oven, 190°C (375°F), Gas Mark 5, for 35 to 40 minutes. Turn onto a wire rack to cool.

To make the caraque, melt the chocolate on a plate over a pan of hot water. Spread thinly on a board and leave until nearly set, then shave it off into curls with a sharp knife.

Make the butter cream as for Gâteau Moka (page 47), flavouring with the melted chocolate instead of coffee essence.

Split the cake in half, sandwich together with some of the butter cream and use the rest to cover the cake. Decorate with the chocolate.
Makes one 23 cm (9 inch) gâteau

Gâteau Pithiviers

75 g (3 oz) ground
  almonds
75 g (3 oz) caster
  sugar
40 g (1 ½ oz) butter
  or margarine
1 egg
25 g (1 oz) plain
  flour, sifted
½ teaspoon almond
  essence
368 g (13 oz) packet
  frozen puff pastry,
  thawed
TO GLAZE:
1 egg white
1 tablespoon caster
  sugar

Mix the almonds with the sugar, fat and egg and beat well. Stir in the flour and almond essence.

Roll out the pastry and cut into two 20 cm (8 inch) rounds, one slightly thicker than the other. Place the thin round on a dampened baking sheet and cover with the almond filling, leaving a 2.5 cm (1 inch) border. Dampen the edge of the pastry and place the thicker round on top. Press the edges together and knock up with the back of a knife.

Decorate with curved cuts in the shape of a wheel. Brush with egg white and sprinkle with the caster sugar. Bake in a preheated hot oven, 220°C (425°F), Gas Mark 7, for 25 to 30 minutes. Transfer to a wire rack to cool.

Makes one 20 cm (8 inch) gâteau

Gâteau aux Fraises

3 eggs, separated
125 g (4 oz) caster
  sugar
grated rind and juice
  of ½ lemon
50 g (2 oz) semolina
25 g (1 oz) ground
  almonds

TO FINISH:
284 ml (10 fl oz)
  double cream,
  whipped
250 g (8 oz)
  strawberries,
  halved
4 tablespoons
  redcurrant jelly
2 teaspoons water
50 g (2 oz) almonds,
  chopped and
  browned

Cream the egg yolks with the sugar,
lemon rind and juice until thick. Stir
in the semolina and ground almonds,
then fold in the stiffly whisked egg
whites. Turn the mixture into a
lined, greased and floured 23 cm
(9 inch) moule a manqué tin and
bake in a preheated moderate oven,
180°C (350°F), Gas Mark 4, for 35 to
40 minutes. Turn onto a wire rack to
cool.

Split the cake in half and sandwich
together with three-quarters of the
cream. Arrange the strawberries on
the top.

Heat the redcurrant jelly with the
water, sieve, reheat and use to glaze
the strawberries and side of the cake.
Press the browned almonds around
the side and pipe the remaining
cream around the top to decorate.

Makes one 23 cm (9 inch) gâteau

Gâteau Moka

GENOESE SPONGE:
50 g (2 oz) butter
4 eggs
125 g (4 oz) caster
sugar
125 g (4 oz) plain
flour, sifted
BUTTER CREAM:
2 egg whites
125 g (4 oz) icing
sugar, sifted
125 g (4 oz)
unsalted butter
1 tablespoon coffee
essence
TO DECORATE:
125 g (4 oz) flaked
almonds
icing sugar

Prepare and bake the sponge as for Genoese Sponge (page 12).

To make the butter cream, whisk the egg whites and icing sugar together over a pan of simmering water until the mixture holds its shape. Cool slightly. Cream the butter until soft, then add the meringue mixture a little at a time. Flavour with the coffee essence.

Split the sponge in half and sandwich together with some of the butter cream.

Spread the remaining butter cream all over the cake and decorate with the almonds. Sift a little icing sugar over the top.

Makes one 23 cm (9 inch) gâteau

Caramel Chip Gâteau

125 g (4 oz) butter
or margarine
175 g (6 oz) soft
brown sugar
3 eggs
250 g (8 oz)
self-raising flour,
sifted
4 tablespoons hot
black coffee
CARAMEL CHIPS:
175 g (6 oz) caster
sugar
FILLING:
50 g (2 oz) butter
125 g (4 oz) icing
sugar, sifted
2 tablespoons milk
ICING:
350 g (12 oz) icing
sugar, sifted
1 tablespoon coffee
essence
2 tablespoons water

Cream the fat until soft then add the sugar and beat thoroughly. Add the eggs one at a time, adding a tablespoon of flour with each one.

Fold in the remaining flour with the coffee, then turn into two lined and greased 20 cm (8 inch) sandwich tins. Bake in a preheated moderate oven, 180°C (350°F), Gas Mark 4, for 25 to 30 minutes. Turn onto a wire rack to cool.

To make the caramel chips, place the sugar in a small pan and heat gently until dissolved. Boil until it forms a golden brown caramel and pour immediately onto a greased baking sheet. When cool, break the caramel into small pieces. Set aside about half for decorating. Crush the remainder finely with a rolling pin.

To make the filling, cream the butter and icing sugar together, add a tablespoon of finely crushed caramel and mix to a soft consistency with the milk. Use to sandwich the cakes together.

To make the icing, mix the icing sugar with the coffee essence and water. Pour over the cake and decorate with the remaining caramel chips.

Makes one 20 cm (8 inch) gâteau

Gâteau aux Noisettes

125 g (4 oz) caster
  sugar
3 eggs
50 g (2 oz) plain
  flour, sifted
50 g (2 oz) ground
  hazelnuts,
  browned
1 tablespoon oil
BUTTER CREAM:
2 egg whites
125 g (4 oz) icing
  sugar
125 g (4 oz)
  unsalted butter
1 tablespoon coffee
  essence
PRALINE POWDER:
50 g (2 oz)
  unblanched
  almonds
50 g (2 oz) caster
  sugar
ICING:
175 g (6 oz) icing
  sugar, sifted
2 teaspoons coffee
  essence
2 teaspoons water

Whisk the sugar and eggs together in a bowl until thick enough to leave a trail. Fold in the flour, hazelnuts and oil.

Turn into a lined and greased 23 cm (9 inch) moule a manqué tin and bake in a preheated moderately hot oven, 190°C (375°F), Gas Mark 5, for 25 to 30 minutes until the cake springs back when lightly pressed. Turn onto a wire rack to cool, then split in half.

Make the butter cream as for Gâteau Moka (page 47) and the praline powder as for Apricot Gâteau (page 51).

Mix 2 tablespoons praline into the butter cream. Use 3 tablespoons of this to sandwich the sponge together. Spread more butter cream around the side of the cake and press the remaining praline onto it.

For the icing, mix the icing sugar with the coffee essence and water until smooth. Spread over the top of the cake and leave to set.

Pipe the remaining butter cream in a border around the top edge.
Makes one 23 cm (9 inch) gâteau

Coffee and Walnut Layer Cake

4 eggs
175 g (6 oz) caster
  sugar
125 g (4 oz) plain
  flour, sifted
1 tablespoon oil
125 g (4 oz)
  walnuts, finely
  chopped
BUTTER ICING:
250 g (8 oz) butter
500 g (1 lb) icing
  sugar, sifted
2 tablespoons milk
2 tablespoons coffee
  essence
TO DECORATE:
walnut halves

Line and grease two 20 cm (8 inch) sandwich tins. Whisk the eggs and sugar in a bowl over a pan of boiling water until thick enough to leave a trail. (If using an electric beater, the hot water is unnecessary.)

Partially fold in the flour, then add the oil and chopped walnuts and fold in gently. Divide between the prepared tins and bake in a preheated moderately hot oven, 190°C (375°F), Gas Mark 5, for 30 to 35 minutes until the cakes spring back when lightly pressed. Turn onto a wire rack to cool. Split each cake in half.

To make the butter icing, cream the fat with half the icing sugar until soft, then add the milk, essence and remaining icing sugar. Beat well.

Spread a quarter of the icing onto three of the cake rounds and sandwich the cake together. Swirl the remaining icing over the cake and decorate with walnut halves.
Makes one 20 cm (8 inch) cake

Apricot Gâteau

SPONGE:
3 eggs
125 g (4 oz) caster
  sugar
grated rind and juice
  of 1 lemon
50 g (2 oz) semolina
25 g (1 oz) ground
  almonds

PRALINE POWDER:
50 g (2 oz) almonds
  (unblanched)
50 g (2 oz) caster
  sugar

TO FINISH:
170 ml (6 fl oz)
  double cream
411 g (14½ oz) can
  apricot halves
4 tablespoons apricot
  glaze (see page
  54)

Make the sponge as for Gâteau aux Fraises (page 46).

Place the unblanched almonds and sugar in a pan and heat very gently until the sugar melts. Stir with a metal spoon and cook until it is a nut brown colour. Turn onto an oiled baking sheet to cool, then crush to a coarse powder.

Whip the cream and fold in 2 tablespoons of the praline powder. Split the sponge in half and sandwich together with the praline cream. Arrange the apricots on top. Brush the glaze over the apricots and side of the gâteau and press the remaining praline round the side.

Makes one 23 cm (9 inch) gâteau

PÂTISSERIE & SMALL CAKES

Walnut Meringues

2 egg whites
125 g (4 oz) icing
  sugar, sifted
50 g (2 oz) walnuts,
  finely chopped

Whisk the egg whites until stiff and dry. Add the icing sugar a tablespoon at a time and continue to whisk until very thick.

Carefully fold in the walnuts. Place small mounds of the mixture on a baking sheet lined with non-stick paper.

Bake in a preheated moderate oven, 180°C (350°F), Gas Mark 4, for 15 to 20 minutes. Leave to cool slightly, then carefully transfer to a wire rack to cool completely.

Makes 22

Florentines

75 g (3 oz) butter
75 g (3 oz) golden
  syrup
25 g (1 oz) plain
  flour
75 g (3 oz) flaked
  almonds, coarsely
  chopped
25 g (1 oz) chopped
  mixed peel
50 g (2 oz) glacé
  cherries, coarsely
  chopped
1 teaspoon lemon
  juice
125 g (4 oz) plain
  chocolate

Melt the butter and syrup in a small pan, then stir in the flour, almonds, mixed peel, cherries and lemon juice.

Place teaspoonfuls of the mixture well apart on baking sheets lined with non-stick paper. Flatten with a fork and bake in a preheated moderate oven, 180°C (350°F), Gas Mark 4, for 8 to 10 minutes. Transfer to a wire rack to cool.

Melt the chocolate in a bowl over a pan of hot water, then spread over the flat underside of each florentine. Place the biscuits chocolate side up on a wire rack and mark the chocolate into wavy lines with a fork. Leave until set.
Makes 14

Mocha Slices

GENOESE SPONGE:
25 g (1 oz) butter
2 eggs
50 g (2 oz) caster
  sugar
50 g (2 oz) plain
  flour, sifted
BUTTER CREAM:
2 egg whites
125 g (4 oz) icing
  sugar, sifted
125 g (4 oz)
  unsalted butter
1 tablespoon coffee
  essence
APRICOT GLAZE:
4 tablespoons apricot
  jam
3 tablespoons water
squeeze of lemon
  juice
ICING:
250 g (8 oz) icing
  sugar, sifted
2 teaspoons coffee
  essence
1 ½ tablespoons
  water

Prepare the sponge as for Genoese Sponge (page 12). Turn into a lined and greased 18 cm (7 inch) square shallow tin and bake in a preheated moderately hot oven, 190°C (375°F), Gas Mark 5, for 25 to 30 minutes. Turn onto a wire rack to cool, then split in half.

Prepare the butter cream as for Gâteau Moka (page 47), and use some to sandwich the cake together. Cut the cake into fingers, 7.5 x 2.5 cm (3 x 1 inch).

To make the apricot glaze, heat the jam and water in a small pan and boil for 3 to 4 minutes. Add the lemon juice, sieve, then reheat and brush over the fingers to coat completely. Leave to set.

To make the icing, combine the icing sugar, coffee essence and water, then spread over the fingers and leave to set.

Pipe the remaining butter cream along the middle of each slice.

Makes 10

Langues de Chats

50 g (2 oz) butter
50 g (2 oz) caster
  sugar
2 egg whites
50 g (2 oz) plain
  flour, sifted
vanilla essence

Cream the butter and sugar together until light and fluffy. Whisk the egg whites lightly and gradually beat into the creamed mixture. Carefully fold in the flour and essence.

Place in a piping bag fitted with a 1 cm (⅜ inch) plain nozzle and pipe 7.5 cm (3 inch) lengths on a greased and floured baking sheet. Bake in a preheated moderately hot oven, 200°C (400°F), Gas Mark 6, for 10 minutes; the biscuits should be pale golden but darker around the edges. Transfer to a wire rack to cool.

Makes 20 to 24

Viennese Fingers

175 g (6 oz) butter
  or margarine
50 g (2 oz) icing
  sugar
grated rind of
  1 orange
125 g (4 oz) plain
  flour
50 g (2 oz) cornflour
2 tablespoons apricot
  jam
75 g (3 oz) plain
  chocolate

Cream the butter or margarine and sugar together with the orange rind until light and fluffy.

Sift in the flour and cornflour and beat well. Place in a piping bag fitted with a 2.5 cm (1 inch) fluted nozzle, and pipe 7.5 cm (3 inch) fingers well apart on a baking sheet lined with non-stick paper.

Bake in a preheated moderate oven, 180°C (350°F), Gas Mark 4, for 15 minutes. Transfer to a wire rack to cool. Sandwich the fingers together in pairs with a little jam.

Melt the chocolate in a small bowl over a pan of hot water. Dip both ends of the fingers in the chocolate and place on a piece of greaseproof paper. Leave until set.

Makes 12

Japonais

50 g (2 oz) ground
  almonds
125 g (4 oz) caster
  sugar
2 egg whites
BUTTER ICING:
75 g (3 oz) butter
175 g (6 oz) icing
  sugar, sifted
1 teaspoon coffee
  essence
1 tablespoon milk
GLACÉ ICING:
125 g (4 oz) icing
  sugar, sifted
1 teaspoon coffee
  essence
2 teaspoons water
TO FINISH:
25 g (1 oz) ground
  almonds, browned
8 hazelnuts, toasted
  and skinned

Mix the almonds and sugar together
and set aside. Whisk the egg whites
until stiff, then fold in the almonds
and sugar. Spoon the mixture into a
piping bag fitted with a 1 cm
(½ inch) plain nozzle and pipe 16
5 cm (2 inch) rounds on non-stick
paper placed on a baking sheet. Bake
in a preheated cool oven, 150°C
(300°F), Gas Mark 2, for 30 to 35
minutes. Transfer to a wire rack to
cool.

Make the butter icing as for Coffee
Walnut Layer Cake (page 50).
Sandwich the rounds together in
pairs with some of the icing and
spread more round the sides.

To make the glacé icing, mix the
icing sugar with the coffee essence
and water until smooth.

Press ground almonds round the
side of each cake. Place a teaspoon of
the glacé icing on top and spread to
the edge. Leave to set, then decorate
with piped rosettes of the remaining
butter icing and hazelnuts.
Makes 8

Chocolate Éclairs

50 g (2 oz) butter or
   margarine
150 ml (¼ pint)
   water
65 g (2½ oz) plain
   flour, sifted
2 eggs, beaten
170 ml (6 fl oz)
   double cream,
   whipped
ICING:
125 g (4 oz) plain
   chocolate
15 g (½ oz) butter

Melt the butter or margarine in a saucepan over a gentle heat. Add the water and bring to the boil. Remove from the heat, add the flour all at once and beat well until the mixture leaves the sides of the pan clean. Cool slightly, then add the eggs a little at a time, beating well between each addition.

Spoon the mixture into a piping bag fitted with a 1 cm (½ inch) plain nozzle and pipe 7.5 cm (3 inch) lengths onto a dampened baking sheet. Bake in a preheated moderately hot oven, 200°C (400°F), Gas Mark 6, for 25 minutes until crisp and golden brown. Make a slit in the side of each éclair to allow the steam to escape and cool on a wire rack.

Fill a piping bag fitted with a 1 cm (½ inch) plain nozzle with the cream and pipe a little into each éclair.

Melt the chocolate and butter on a plate over a pan of hot water and mix well. Dip each éclair into the chocolate; place on a wire rack to set.
Makes 10 to 12

Tartelettes aux Fraises

PÂTE SUCRÉE:
125 g (4 oz) plain
    flour
50 g (2 oz) butter,
    softened
50 g (2 oz) caster
    sugar
2 egg yolks
few drops of vanilla
    essence
GLAZE:
4 tablespoons
    redcurrant jelly
1 tablespoon water
FILLING:
250 g (8 oz)
    strawberries

Sift the flour onto a board, make a well in the centre and place the butter, sugar, egg yolks and vanilla in the well. Using the fingertips of one hand, work these ingredients together until well blended, then draw in the flour. Knead lightly until smooth and chill for 1 hour.

Roll out the pastry very thinly and use to line 14 patty tins, then press a square of foil into each. Bake blind in a preheated moderately hot oven, 190°C (375°F), Gas Mark 5, for 10 minutes or until golden. Cool, then remove foil and turn out.

To make the glaze, heat the redcurrant jelly with the water. Bring to the boil, then sieve and reheat. Brush the cases with glaze. Arrange the fruit in the cases and brush with the remaining glaze.
Makes 14

Cream Horns

212 g (7½ oz)
    packet frozen puff
    pastry, thawed
beaten egg to glaze
strawberry jam
170 ml (6 fl oz)
    double cream,
    whipped
TO DECORATE:
cherries and angelica
icing sugar

Roll out the pastry into a rectangle about 25 x 33 cm (10 x 13 inches) and trim the edges. Cut into 10 strips 2.5 cm (1 inch) wide. Dampen one long edge of each strip with water and wind round 10 cornet moulds, starting at the point and overlapping the dampened edge. Gently press the edges together. Place on a dampened baking sheet and chill for 15 minutes.

Brush with egg and bake in a preheated hot oven, 220°C (425°F), Gas Mark 7, for 15 to 20 minutes until golden brown. Leave for 5 minutes before carefully removing the moulds. Cool on a wire rack.

Spoon a little jam into each horn then pipe in the cream. Decorate with a piece of cherry and angelica and sprinkle with icing sugar.
Makes 10

Walnut Barquettes

PÂTE SUCRÉE:
125 g (4 oz) plain flour
50g (2 oz) butter, softened
50 g (2 oz) caster sugar
2 egg yolks
few drops vanilla essence

WALNUT FILLING:
50 g (2 oz) butter
50 g (2 oz) caster sugar
1 egg, beaten
25 g (1 oz) plain flour, sifted
50 g (2 oz) walnuts, ground

ICING:
125 g (4 oz) icing sugar, sifted
1 egg white

Make the pâte sucrée as for Tartelettes aux Fraises (opposite). Roll out thinly and use to line 14 barquette moulds. Prick and chill for 20 minutes.

To make the walnut filling, cream the butter and sugar together until light and fluffy, then add the egg and flour and beat well. Fold in the walnuts, spoon the mixture into a piping bag fitted with a plain nozzle and pipe into the pastry cases.

To make the icing, mix the icing sugar with the egg white until smooth. Spoon into a piping bag fitted with a writing nozzle and pipe a criss-cross pattern over each cake.

Bake in a preheated moderately hot oven, 200°C (400°F), Gas Mark 6, for 20 minutes. Leave in the moulds for 5 minutes, then transfer to a wire rack to cool.
Makes 14

Brandy Snaps

125 g (4 oz) butter
125 g (4 oz)
  demerara sugar
125 g (4 oz) golden
  syrup
125 g (4 oz) plain
  flour
1 teaspoon ground
  ginger

Put the butter, sugar and syrup into a saucepan and heat gently until the butter has melted and the sugar dissolved. Cool slightly, then sift in the flour and ginger and beat well.

Place teaspoonfuls of the mixture on a greased baking sheet at least 10 cm (4 inches) apart. Bake in a preheated moderate oven, 180°C (350°F), Gas Mark 4, for 10 to 12 minutes until golden.

Leave to cool slightly then remove with a palette knife and roll round the greased handle of a wooden spoon. Leave for 1 to 2 minutes to set, then slip them off carefully onto a wire rack to cool. Serve plain or filled with whipped cream.

Makes 35

NOTE: If the biscuits cool too much and are too brittle to roll, return to the oven for 1 minute to soften.

Frangipane Tartlets

SHORTCRUST
PASTRY:
25g (1 oz) butter
25g (1 oz) lard
*125g (4 oz) plain
flour, sifted*
water to mix
FILLING:
50 g (2 oz) butter
*50 g (2 oz) caster
sugar*
1 egg, beaten
1 tablespoon flour
*50 g (2 oz) ground
almonds*
*2 drops of almond
essence*
*25 g (1 oz) flaked
almonds*
*2 tablespoons apricot
glaze (see page 21)*

To make the pastry, rub the fat into
the flour until the mixture resembles
breadcrumbs. Stir in enough water
to make a firm dough. Knead lightly,
cover and chill for 30 minutes.

Roll out thinly, cut into ten 7.5 cm
(3 inch) circles and use to line 10
deep patty tins. Chill for 15 minutes.

Cream the butter and sugar
together until light and fluffy, add
the egg, then beat in the flour. Mix
in the almonds and essence, then
spoon into a piping bag fitted with a
1 cm (½ inch) plain nozzle and
two-thirds fill the pastry cases.
Sprinkle with flaked almonds and
bake in a preheated moderately hot
oven, 200°C (400°F), Gas Mark 6, for
20 minutes. Transfer to a wire rack
then brush with the glaze.
Makes 10

Sponge Fingers

50 g (2 oz) caster
   sugar
2 eggs
vanilla essence
50 g (2 oz) plain
   flour, sifted
caster sugar for
   dredging

Whisk the sugar, eggs and vanilla
essence in a mixing bowl over a pan
of hot water until thick. (If using an
electric beater, the hot water is
unnecessary.) Fold in the flour.

Place the mixture in a piping bag
fitted with a 1 cm (½ inch) plain
nozzle and pipe into finger lengths
on greased and floured baking sheets.
Dust well with caster sugar and bake
in a preheated moderately hot oven,
190°C (375°F), Gas Mark 5, for 6 to 8
minutes until golden brown.
Transfer to a wire rack to cool.
Makes 22

Almond Curls

75 g (3 oz) butter
75 g (3 oz) caster
   sugar
50 g (2 oz) plain
   flour, sifted
75 g (3 oz) flaked
   almonds

Cream the butter and sugar together
until light and fluffy. Stir in the flour
and almonds and mix well. Place
teaspoonfuls of the mixture well
apart on a greased baking sheet and
flatten with a damp fork.

Bake in a preheated moderately
hot oven, 200°C (400°F), Gas Mark
6, for 6 to 8 minutes until pale
golden. Leave on the baking sheet
for 1 minute, then remove with a
palette knife and place on a rolling
pin to curl. Leave until set in a curl,
then remove very carefully.
Makes 25

Tea-Time Truffles

300 g (10 oz) cake
   crumbs
50 g (2 oz) caster
   sugar
2 tablespoons cocoa
3 tablespoons apricot
   jam
1 tablespoon rum
4 tablespoons choco-
   late vermicelli

Mix the cake crumbs, sugar and
cocoa together in a bowl. Add the
jam and rum and mix to a stiff paste.
Form into balls the size of a walnut
and roll in the chocolate vermicelli.
Serve in paper cases.
Makes 15

Strawberry Palmiers

212 g (7½ oz)
    packet frozen puff
    pastry, thawed
75 g (3 oz) sugar
170 ml (6 fl oz)
    double cream,
    whipped
50 g (2 oz)
    strawberries,
    halved
icing sugar for
    dredging

Roll out the pastry on a well sugared surface to a rectangle about 30 x 25 cm (12 x 10 inches).

Sprinkle with the sugar and press it in with a rolling pin. Take the shorter edge of the pastry and roll it up to the centre. Roll the other side to meet it at the centre. Moisten with water and press together to join the rolls. Cut into 1 cm (½ inch) slices and place well apart, cut side down on a dampened baking sheet, flattening them slightly.

Bake in a preheated hot oven, 220°C (425°F), Gas Mark 7, for 12 to 15 minutes; turn the palmiers over when they begin to brown, so that both sides caramelize. Transfer to a wire rack to cool. Spoon the cream into a piping bag fitted with a 1 cm (½ inch) fluted nozzle and pipe swirls of cream onto half of the palmiers. Arrange a few strawberries on the cream and top with the remaining palmiers. Press down and sprinkle with icing sugar.
Makes 6

Mille Feuilles

212 g (7½ oz)
packet frozen puff
pastry, thawed
125 g (4 oz) icing
sugar, sifted
1 tablespoon water
3 tablespoons
redcurrant jelly
3 tablespoons
strawberry jam
170 ml (6 fl oz)
double cream,
whipped

Roll out the pastry into a large thin sheet, prick all over and cut into 15 pieces 10 x 6 cm (4 x 2½ inches). Place on dampened baking sheets and chill for 15 minutes.

Bake in a preheated hot oven, 220°C (425°F), Gas Mark 7, for 8 to 10 minutes until dark golden brown. Transfer to a wire rack to cool then split each piece in half.

Mix the icing sugar with the water to make a smooth icing and spread over the underside of 10 pastry slices. Place the redcurrant jelly in a piping bag fitted with a 5 mm (¼ inch) plain nozzle and pipe lines horizontally across the icing at 1 cm (½ inch) intervals. Take a skewer and draw it across from left to right and right to left in alternate lines to achieve a marbled effect. Set aside.

Cover another 10 pastry pieces with jam and cream. Place the remaining pastry pieces on top and cover with more jam and cream. Top with the iced pastry and press down firmly.
Makes 10

BREADS & TEABREADS

Soda Bread

1 kg (2 lb) plain
    flour
2 teaspoons salt
1 teaspoon
    bicarbonate of soda
1 teaspoon cream of
    tartar
50 g (2 oz) butter or
    margarine
600 ml (1 pint)
    buttermilk
flour for sprinkling

Sift the dry ingredients into a mixing
bowl and rub in the fat. Add the
buttermilk and mix quickly to a soft
dough. Turn onto a floured surface,
knead lightly and divide in half.
Shape each half into a round about 5
cm (2 inches) thick and place on a
floured baking sheet. Cut a deep
cross on the top of each loaf and
sprinkle with flour.

Bake in a preheated hot oven,
220°C (425°F), Gas Mark 7, for 25 to
30 minutes. Transfer to a wire rack
to cool.

Makes two 500 g (1 lb) loaves

Malt Loaf

550 g (1 lb 2 oz)
plain flour
1 teaspoon salt
50 g (2 oz) soft
brown sugar
125 g (4 oz) currants
125 g (4 oz)
sultanas
25 g (1 oz) chopped
mixed peel
25 g (1 oz) fresh
yeast
250 ml (8 fl oz)
warm milk
50 g (2 oz) butter or
margarine
4 tablespoons malt
extract
2 tablespoons clear
honey to glaze

Place all the dry ingredients in a bowl. Cream the yeast with a little of the milk and set aside. Add the fat and malt extract to the remaining milk and heat until melted. Cool slightly, then add to the dry ingredients with the yeast.

Beat to a soft dough, cover with a damp cloth and leave to rise in a warm place until doubled in size. Turn out and knead for 5 minutes until smooth. Divide in half and place in two 500 g (1 lb) greased loaf tins. Cover and leave in a warm place for about 1 hour until the dough reaches the top of the tins.

Bake in a preheated moderately hot oven, 190°C (375°F), Gas Mark 5, for 35 to 40 minutes until the bread sounds hollow when tapped. Turn onto a wire rack, then brush with honey.

Makes two 500 g (1 lb) loaves

Wholewheat Soda Bread

250 g (8 oz) plain
  flour
1 teaspoon
  bicarbonate of soda
2 teaspoons cream of
  tartar
2 teaspoons salt
350 g (12 oz)
  wholewheat flour
300 ml (½ pint)
  milk
4 tablespoons water
plain flour for
  sprinkling

Sift the dry ingredients into a mixing bowl. Mix in the wholewheat flour then add the milk and water and mix to a soft dough. Turn onto a floured surface, knead lightly, then shape into a large round about 5 cm (2 inches) thick. Place on a floured baking sheet, cut a deep cross on the top of the loaf and sprinkle with flour. Bake in a preheated hot oven, 220°C (425°F), Gas Mark 7, for 25 to 30 minutes. Transfer to a wire rack to cool.

Makes one 20 cm (8 inch) loaf

Granary Bread

500 g (1 lb) granary
  flour
1 teaspoon salt
15 g (½ oz) fresh
  yeast
300 ml (½ pint)
  warm water
1 tablespoon malt
  extract
1 tablespoon oil
cracked wheat

Mix the flour and salt in a bowl. Cream the yeast with a little of the water and leave until frothy. Add to the flour with the remaining water, malt extract and oil and mix to a dough.

Turn onto a floured surface and knead for 5 minutes until smooth and elastic. Place in a clean bowl, cover with a damp cloth and leave in a warm place to rise until doubled in size. Turn onto a floured surface and knead for 2 minutes. Shape into a round and place on a greased baking sheet. Brush with water and sprinkle with cracked wheat. Cover and leave in a warm place for about 30 minutes, until almost doubled in size.

Bake in a preheated hot oven, 220°C (425°F), Gas Mark 7, for 35 minutes, or until it sounds hollow when tapped. Cool on a wire rack.
Makes one loaf

Wholewheat Bread

1.5 kg (3 lb)
  wholewheat flour
1 tablespoon salt
25 g (1 oz) butter
25 g (1 oz) fresh
  yeast
900 ml – 1.2 litres
  (1½–2 pints)
  warm water
2 tablespoons malt
  extract
1 tablespoon cracked
  wheat

Mix the flour and salt together and rub in the butter. Mix the yeast with a little of the water and leave for 10 minutes. Mix the malt extract with the remaining water, add to the flour with the yeast and mix to a smooth dough.

Turn onto a floured surface and knead for 8 to 10 minutes until smooth and elastic. Place in a clean bowl, cover with a damp cloth and leave to rise in a warm place for about 2 hours until doubled in size.

Turn onto a floured surface, knead for a few minutes then divide into 4 pieces and place in greased 500 g (1 lb) loaf tins or clean greased clay flower pots. Brush with water and sprinkle with cracked wheat.

Cover and leave in a warm place for about 30 minutes until the dough just reaches the top of the tins. Bake in a preheated hot oven, 220°C (425°F), Gas Mark 7, for 30 to 40 minutes, or until the bread sounds hollow when tapped. Transfer to a wire rack to cool.
Makes four 500 g (1 lb) loaves

Basic White Bread

25 g (1 oz) fresh
  yeast
1 teaspoon caster
  sugar
900 ml (1½ pints)
  warm water
1.5 kg (3 lb) plain
  flour
1 tablespoon salt
1 tablespoon oil
flour for sprinkling

Cream the yeast with the sugar and a little of the water and leave for 10 minutes. Sift the flour and salt into a mixing bowl. Make a well in the centre and pour in the yeast, remaining water and oil. Mix to a smooth dough.

Turn onto a floured surface and knead for 8 to 10 minutes until smooth and elastic. Place in a clean bowl, cover with a damp cloth and leave to rise in a warm place for about 2 hours until doubled in size.

Turn onto a floured surface, knead for a few minutes, then divide in half and place in two greased 1 kg (2 lb) loaf tins. Make a cut along each loaf. Alternatively shape into rounds or cottage loaves and place on a floured baking sheet. Cover and leave in a warm place for 30 minutes until risen to the top of the tins.

Sprinkle with flour and bake in a preheated hot oven, 220°C (425°F), Gas Mark 7, for 35 to 40 minutes or until the bread sounds hollow when tapped. Cool on a wire rack.

Makes two 1 kg (2 lb) loaves

Milk Rolls

300 ml (½ pint)
  milk
50 g (2 oz) butter or
  margarine
15 g (½ oz) fresh
  yeast
1 teaspoon caster
  sugar
500 g (1 lb) plain
  flour
1 teaspoon salt
1 small egg, beaten
TO FINISH:
beaten egg
poppy seeds

Place the milk and fat in a pan and heat until lukewarm. Cream the yeast and sugar together, add a little of the warm milk and leave until frothy.

Sift the flour and salt into a warm bowl. Make a well in the centre and pour in the yeast, milk mixture and egg. Mix to a soft dough, then knead well until smooth and elastic.

Place in a clean bowl, cover with a damp cloth and leave to rise in a warm place for about 30 minutes until doubled in size. Turn onto a well-floured surface and knead for 2 to 3 minutes. Cut into 14 pieces and shape into rolls.

Place on a greased baking sheet, cover and leave in a warm place until doubled in size, about 10 to 15 minutes. Glaze with beaten egg, sprinkle with poppy seeds and bake in a preheated hot oven, 220°C (425°F), Gas Mark 7, for 20 minutes. Cool on a wire rack.
Makes 14

Hot Cross Buns

500 g (1 lb) plain
   flour
1 teaspoon salt
1 teaspoon ground
   mixed spice
2 teaspoons ground
   cinnamon
50 g (2 oz) soft
   brown sugar
50 g (2 oz) butter or
   margarine
25 g (1 oz) yeast
175 ml (6 fl oz)
   warm milk
1 large egg
75 g (3 oz) currants
25 g (1 oz) chopped
   mixed peel
PASTE:
3 tablespoons plain
   flour
2 tablespoons milk
1 teaspoon oil
GLAZE:
2 tablespoons milk
2 tablespoons caster
   sugar

Sift the flour, salt, spices and sugar into a mixing bowl and rub in the fat. Cream the yeast with a little of the milk and leave until frothy. Make a well in the centre of the dry ingredients, pour in the yeast, add the egg, fruit and remaining milk and mix together to make a smooth dough.

Turn onto a floured surface and knead for 8 minutes until smooth and elastic. Place in a clean bowl, cover with a damp cloth and leave to rise in a warm place for about 2 hours until doubled in size. Turn onto a floured surface and knead for 2 minutes. Divide into 12 pieces, shape into buns and place on a greased baking sheet. Cover and leave in a warm place for about 25 minutes until doubled in size.

To make the paste, put the flour in a small bowl and gradually stir in the milk and oil to make a smooth thick batter. Spoon into a small piping bag fitted with a 5 mm (¼ inch) plain nozzle and pipe a cross on the top of each bun. Bake in a preheated moderately hot oven, 200°C (400°F), Gas Mark 6, for 20 minutes until golden brown.

Place the milk and sugar in a small pan, bring to the boil and simmer for 2 minutes. Brush the buns with the glaze as soon as they come out of the oven. Transfer to a wire rack and cool slightly before serving.
Makes 12

Irish Brack

500 g (1 lb) mixed
  fruit
200 g (7 oz) soft
  brown sugar
300 ml (½ pint) cold
  tea
1 egg, beaten
275 g (9 oz)
  self-raising flour

Put the fruit, sugar and tea in a bowl and leave for 3 hours or until the tea is absorbed. Beat in the egg and flour.

Pour into a lined and greased 1 kg (2 lb) loaf tin and bake in a preheated moderate oven, 180°C (350°F), Gas Mark 4, for 1½ to 2 hours. Leave in the tin for 5 minutes, then cool on a wire rack. Serve sliced, with butter.
Makes one 1 kg (2 lb) loaf

Fig Loaf

250 g (8 oz) dried
  figs, chopped
125 g (4 oz) soft
  brown sugar
250 g (8 oz)
  All-Bran
2 tablespoons black
  treacle
600 ml (1 pint) cold
  tea
4 teaspoons baking
  powder
250 g (8 oz)
  wholewheat flour

Place the figs, sugar, All-Bran, treacle and tea in a mixing bowl and leave to stand for 1 hour. Sift in the baking powder, add the flour and mix together thoroughly.

Turn into a lined and greased 1 kg (2 lb) loaf tin and bake in a preheated moderate oven, 180°C (350°F), Gas Mark 4, for 1¼ to 1½ hours.

Turn onto a wire rack to cool. Serve sliced, with butter.
Makes one 1 kg (2 lb) loaf

Date Loaf

250 g (8 oz) dates,
  chopped
175 ml (6 fl oz) cold
  tea
250 g (8 oz)
  wholewheat flour
4 teaspoons baking
  powder
1 teaspoon ground
  mixed spice
175 g (6 oz) soft
  brown sugar
1 egg
TOPPING:
1 tablespoon
  demerara sugar

Put the dates in a bowl, pour over the tea and leave to soak for 2 hours. Add the remaining ingredients and mix thoroughly.

Turn into a lined and greased 1 kg (2 lb) loaf tin. Sprinkle with the demerara sugar and bake in a preheated moderate oven, 180°C (350°F), Gas Mark 4, for 1 to 1¼ hours.

Leave in the tin for 5 minutes, then turn onto a wire rack to cool. Serve sliced, spread with butter.
Makes one 1 kg (2 lb) loaf

Bran Bread

125 g (4 oz)
   All-Bran
75 g (3 oz) soft
   brown sugar
125 g (4 oz) mixed
   dried fruit
300 ml (½ pint)
   milk
125 g (4 oz) self-
   raising flour, sifted

Place the All-Bran, sugar, fruit and milk in a mixing bowl and leave to stand for 1 hour. Mix in the flour.

Turn into a lined and greased 500 g (1 lb) loaf tin and bake in a preheated moderate oven, 180°C (350°F), Gas Mark 4, for 55 to 60 minutes. Turn onto a wire rack to cool. Serve sliced, with butter.
Makes one 500 g (1 lb) loaf

Banana and Walnut Loaf

250 g (8 oz)
   self-raising flour
½ teaspoon ground
   cinnamon
125 g (4 oz) butter
   or margarine
125 g (4 oz) soft
   brown sugar
2 large eggs
3 large bananas,
   mashed
75 g (3 oz) walnuts,
   chopped

Grease and line a 1 kg (2 lb) loaf tin. Sift the flour with the cinnamon.

Cream the fat and sugar together until light and fluffy. Beat in the eggs one at a time, then the bananas. Fold in the flour and walnuts.

Pour into the prepared tin and bake in a preheated moderate oven, 180°C (350°F), Gas Mark 4, for 1 to 1¼ hours. Leave in the tin for 2 minutes then turn onto a wire rack to cool. Serve sliced, with butter.
Makes one 1 kg (2 lb) loaf

Ginger and Cherry Loaf

175 g (6 oz) plain
   flour
1½ teaspoons baking
   powder
2 teaspoons ground
   ginger
75 g (3 oz) butter
50 g (2 oz)
   crystallized
   ginger, chopped
75 g (3 oz) glacé
   cherries, chopped
75 g (3 oz) soft
   brown sugar
6 tablespoons milk

Sift the dry ingredients into a mixing bowl and rub in the fat until the mixture resembles breadcrumbs. Stir in the chopped ginger, cherries and sugar, then add the milk and mix to a stiff dough.

Turn into a greased and lined 500 g (1 lb) loaf tin and bake in a preheated moderate oven, 180°C (350°F), Gas Mark 4, for 1 to 1¼ hours. Turn onto a wire rack to cool. Serve sliced, with butter.
Makes one 500 g (1 lb) loaf

Fruit Plait

ENRICHED DOUGH:
*250 g (8 oz) plain
   flour*
½ teaspoon salt
*15 g (½ oz) fresh
   yeast*
*6 tablespoons warm
   milk*
*50 g (2 oz) butter or
   margarine*
1 egg, beaten
*50 g (2 oz) caster
   sugar*
FILLING:
*500 g (1 lb) apples,
   peeled, cored and
   chopped*
*125 g (4 oz)
   sultanas*
*125 g (4 oz) soft
   brown sugar*
*1 teaspoon ground
   mixed spice*
ICING:
*75 g (3 oz) icing
   sugar*
1 teaspoon water

Sift the flour and salt into a mixing bowl. Cream the yeast with a little of the milk. Melt the fat and add to the flour with the yeast, egg, sugar and remaining milk and mix to a smooth dough. Turn onto a floured surface and knead for 10 minutes until smooth and elastic. Place in a bowl, cover with a damp cloth and leave in a warm place for about 2 hours until doubled in size.

Meanwhile, prepare the filling. Place all the ingredients in a saucepan and cook until pulpy. Turn onto a plate and leave to cool.

Turn the dough onto a floured surface and knead for 2 minutes. Roll into an oblong 35 x 20 cm (14 x 8 inches) and spread the filling down the centre 7.5 cm (3 inches). Make slanting cuts 5 cm (2 inches) long at 2.5 cm (1 inch) intervals at each side of the filling. Take a strip from each side and cross them over the filling to make a plait. Tuck the last two strips underneath and seal with water.

Place on a greased baking sheet. Cover and leave in a warm place for about 30 minutes until doubled in size. Bake in a preheated moderately hot oven, 200°C (400°F), Gas Mark 6, for 30 to 35 minutes. Transfer to a wire rack to cool.

Mix the icing sugar with the water and brush over the plait while still warm.

Makes one 35 cm (14 inch) plait

Coconut Loaf

125 g (4 oz) butter
   or margarine
125 g (4 oz) caster
   sugar
2 eggs
175 g (6 oz)
   self-raising flour,
   sifted
4 tablespoons
   desiccated coconut
2 tablespoons milk

Cream the fat and sugar together until light and fluffy. Beat in the eggs one at a time, adding a little of the flour with the second. Fold in the remaining flour, 3 tablespoons of the coconut and the milk.

Turn into a lined and greased 500 g (1 lb) loaf tin and sprinkle with the remaining coconut. Bake in a preheated moderate oven, 180°C (350°F), Gas Mark 4, for 1 to 1¼ hours. Turn out and cool on a wire rack.

Makes one 500 g (1 lb) loaf

Swedish Tea Ring

ENRICHED DOUGH:
250 g (8 oz) plain
  flour
1/2 teaspoon salt
15 g (1/2 oz) fresh
  yeast
6 tablespoons warm
  milk
50 g (2 oz) butter
1 egg, beaten
50 g (2 oz) caster
  sugar

FILLING:
50 g (2 oz) butter,
  softened
75 g (3 oz) demerara
  sugar
50 g (2 oz) glacé
  cherries, chopped
50 g (2 oz) raisins
1 teaspoon ground
  cinnamon

DECORATION:
125 g (4 oz) icing
  sugar
1 tablespoon lemon
  juice
25 g (1 oz) walnuts
25 g (1 oz) glacé
  cherries
15 g (1/2 oz) angelica

Make the enriched dough as for Fruit Plait (page 78) and leave to rise until doubled in size.

Turn onto a floured surface and knead for 2 minutes, then roll out to 25 x 46 cm (10 x 18 inches).

Spread with the softened butter, then sprinkle with the sugar, fruit and cinnamon. Roll up tightly from the long side, dampen the edges and seal together well. Place on a greased baking sheet with the seam underneath and form into a ring, joining the ends together. Using scissors, make slanting cuts two-thirds through the ring at 2.5 cm (1 inch) intervals and turn each section on its side.

Cover and leave in a warm place for about 30 minutes until doubled in size, then bake in a preheated moderately hot oven, 200°C (400°F), Gas Mark 6, for 30 minutes. Transfer to a wire rack to cool.

Mix the icing sugar with the lemon juice and pour over the ring while still warm. Decorate with the walnuts, cherries and angelica.
Makes one tea ring

Chelsea Buns

ENRICHED DOUGH:
250 g (8 oz) plain
  flour
½ teaspoon salt
15 g (½ oz) fresh
  yeast
90 ml (3 fl oz)
  warm milk
50 g (2 oz) butter or
  margarine
1 egg, beaten
50 g (2 oz) caster
  sugar
FILLING:
50 g (2 oz) butter or
  margarine
50 g (2 oz) demerara
  sugar
125 g (4 oz) currants
1 teaspoon ground
  mixed spice
GLAZE:
3 tablespoons caster
  sugar
3 tablespoons water

Make the enriched dough as for Fruit Plait (page 78) and leave to rise until doubled in size. Turn onto a floured surface and knead for 2 minutes, then roll out to 30 x 23 cm (12 x 9 inches).

Melt the fat and brush over the dough, then sprinkle with the demerara sugar, fruit and spice. Roll up lengthwise like a Swiss roll, ending with the join underneath. Cut into 9 pieces and place cut side downwards in a greased 18 cm (7 inch) square cake tin.

Cover and leave in a warm place for 20 minutes until almost doubled in size. Bake in a preheated moderately hot oven, 200°C (400°F), Gas Mark 6, for 20 to 25 minutes until golden.

Meanwhile, dissolve the caster sugar in the water, then boil for 2 minutes. Brush the buns as soon as they come out of the oven. Transfer to a wire rack to cool.
Makes 9

FESTIVE & NOVELTY CAKES

Chocolate Log

SWISS ROLL:
3 large eggs
125 g (4 oz) caster
  sugar
50 g (2 oz) plain
  flour
25 g (1 oz) cocoa
1 tablespoon hot
  water

FUDGE ICING:
75 g (3 oz) butter
3 tablespoons milk
2 tablespoons cocoa
300 g (10 oz) icing
  sugar

TO FINISH:
icing sugar

Prepare and bake the Swiss roll as for Swiss Roll (page 13), sifting in the cocoa with the flour. Make the fudge icing as for Devil's Food Cake (page 18). Turn the sponge upside down onto sugared greaseproof paper, peel off the lining paper and trim the edges. Roll up with the sugared paper inside and allow to cool. Unroll and remove the paper, spread with some of the warm fudge icing and roll up like a Swiss roll. Leave the rest of the icing to cool.

Cut a short diagonal wedge off one end of the roll and join it to the side of the log with icing to resemble a branch. Place on a cake board. Cover the log with the cooled icing and mark lines with a fork to resemble the bark of a tree. Sprinkle with icing sugar to look like snow and decorate as liked, with a robin, holly, etc.

Makes one chocolate log

Snowman

175 g (6 oz) butter
  or margarine
175 g (6 oz) caster
  sugar
3 eggs
250 g (8 oz)
  self-raising flour
2 tablespoons hot
  water
ICING:
175 g (6 oz) caster
  sugar
1 egg white
2 tablespoons hot
  water
pinch of cream of
  tartar

Prepare the cake mixture as for Victoria Sandwich (page 8). Grease and flour a 300 ml (½ pint) and a 900 ml (1½ pint) pudding basin and fill each with the mixture. Bake in a preheated moderate oven, 160°C (325°F), Gas Mark 3, for 1 to 1¼ hours for the small cake, and 1½ to 1¾ hours for the large one. Turn onto a wire rack to cool.

Put the icing ingredients in a bowl over a pan of hot water and whisk for about 5 minutes until thick. Trim the small cake into a ball shape. Cover both cakes with icing. Place the large cake upside down on a cake board and place the small one on top for the head.

Decorate as desired with hat, scarf, pipe, sweets, etc.

Makes one snowman

Christmas Cake

275 g (9 oz) plain
   flour
1 teaspoon ground
   mixed spice
½ teaspoon grated
   nutmeg
250 g (8 oz) butter
   or margarine
250 g (8 oz) soft
   brown sugar
grated rind of
   1 lemon
1 tablespoon treacle
5 large eggs
75 g (3 oz) ground
   almonds
350 g (12 oz) currants
250 g (8 oz) sultanas
175 g (6 oz) raisins
125 g (4 oz) glacé
   cherries, quartered
75 g (3 oz) chopped
   mixed peel
50 g (2 oz) split
   almonds, chopped
ALMOND PASTE:
500 g (1 lb) ground
   almonds
250 g (8 oz) icing
   sugar
250 g (8 oz) caster
   sugar
1 large egg
2 teaspoons lemon
   juice
4 drops of almond
   essence
4 tablespoons
   warmed, sieved
   apricot jam
ROYAL ICING:
3 egg whites
750 g (1 ½ lb) icing
   sugar, sifted
1 teaspoon lemon
   juice
2 teaspoons glycerine

Prepare a deep 23 cm (9 inch) cake tin as for Boiled Fruit Cake (page 17).

Make the cake as for Dundee Cake (page 16), adding the treacle with the fat and sugar, and the ground and chopped almonds with the fruit.

Turn into the prepared tin and smooth the top. Bake in a preheated cool oven, 150°C (300°F), Gas Mark 2, for 3 to 4 hours; test with a skewer after 3 hours. Leave in the tin for 10 minutes, then turn onto a wire rack to cool.

(If liked, when cold, make a few holes in the top of the cake with a skewer and pour over 2 tablespoons brandy.) Wrap in double greaseproof paper and store in an airtight tin for at least 2 weeks before using.

TO ALMOND PASTE THE CAKE

Mix the almonds and sugars together, add the egg, lemon juice and essence and mix to a smooth pliable paste. Brush the cake with apricot jam.

Roll out just over half the almond paste into a 23 cm (9 inch) circle and place on top of the cake. Roll out the remaining paste into 2 strips the depth and half the circumference of the cake. Place these round the side of the cake and press together. Stand on a cake board and leave in a dry place for 2 to 3 days before icing.

TO ICE THE CAKE

Lightly whisk the egg whites, then add the icing sugar a little at a time, beating well between each addition, until the icing is smooth and stiff enough to form peaks. Beat in the lemon juice and glycerine.

Spread the icing over the cake and draw up into peaks to look like snow. Decorate with holly, robin, etc. as desired.

Makes one 25 cm (10 inch) cake

Drum Cake

125 g (4 oz) butter
  or margarine
125 g (4 oz) caster
  sugar
2 eggs
125 g (4 oz)
  self-raising flour,
  sifted
1 tablespoon hot
  water
BUTTER ICING:
75 g (3 oz) butter
250 g (8 oz) icing
  sugar, sifted
2 tablespoons milk
red food colouring
GLACÉ ICING:
250 g (8 oz) icing
  sugar, sifted
2 tablespoons water
TO DECORATE:
1 teaspoon cocoa
smarties
2 lollipops

Prepare and bake the cake as for Victoria Sandwich (page 8). Make the butter icing as for Coffee Walnut Layer Cake (page 50), adding the colouring instead of the essence. Sandwich the cakes together with icing, stand on a cake board and cover the sides with the remaining butter icing.

To make the glacé icing, mix the icing sugar and water until smooth. Spread three-quarters over the top of the cake and leave to set.

Add the cocoa to the remaining glacé icing and put into a piping bag fitted with a plain writing nozzle. Place 8 smarties around the side of the cake at the top and another 8 at the bottom, midway between those at the top.

Pipe diagonal lines of chocolate icing to join the smarties top to bottom. Place the lollipops on top for drumsticks.

Makes one drum cake

Tennis Cake

250 g (8 oz) butter
or margarine
250 g (8 oz) caster
sugar
4 eggs
250 g (8 oz)
self-raising flour
2 tablespoons hot
water
BUTTER ICING:
75 g (3 oz) butter
250 g (8 oz) icing
sugar, sifted
2 tablespoons milk
green food colouring
GLACÉ ICING:
250 g (8 oz) icing
sugar, sifted
2 tablespoons water
TO DECORATE:
50 g (2 oz)
desiccated coconut
wafers

Line and grease two 18 x 28 cm (7 x 11 inch) Swiss roll tins. Prepare and bake the cakes as for Victoria Sandwich (page 8).

Make the butter icing as for Coffee Walnut Layer Cake (page 50), adding the colouring instead of the essence. Sandwich the cakes together with icing and place on a cake board. Spread the remaining icing over the sides of the cake. Colour the coconut green and press onto the sides.

Make the glacé icing, keep a little aside, colour the rest green and use to coat the top. Leave to set.

Fit a small piping bag with a plain writing nozzle and fill with the white glacé icing. Pipe white lines on the cake as for a tennis court. Cut the wafers into 2.5 cm (1 inch) strips and place across the centre for a net. Put toy figures on court if liked.
Makes one tennis cake

Hedgehog

1 tablespoon cocoa
2 tablespoons hot
   water
125 g (4 oz)
   margarine
125 g (4 oz) caster
   sugar
2 eggs
125 g (4 oz)
   self-raising flour
BUTTER ICING:
2 tablespoons cocoa
3 tablespoons hot
   water
75 g (3 oz) butter
250 g (8 oz) icing
   sugar
TO DECORATE:
50 g (2 oz) shredded
   almonds
3 smarties

Prepare and bake the cake as for
Castle Cake (page 89), using a 20 cm
(8 inch) sandwich tin. Make the icing
as for Devil's Food Cake (page 18).

Cut the cake vertically in half to
make two semi–circles and sandwich
together with some of the icing. To
form the nose, cut 2 diagonal slices
from each side of the front of the
cake and discard. Stand the flat edge
on a cake board and cover the cake
with icing.

Smooth the icing over the nose
and face and fork lines from front to
back over the rest of the 'hedgehog'.
Stick in the almond strips at random
to represent prickles. Use the
smarties for the nose and eyes.

Makes one 'hedgehog'

Castle Cake

25 g (1 oz) cocoa
3 tablespoons hot
 water
175 g (6 oz)
 margarine
175 g (6 oz) caster
 sugar
3 eggs
175 g (6 oz)
 self-raising flour,
 sifted
BUTTER ICING:
2 tablespoons cocoa
3 tablespoons hot
 water
75 g (3 oz) butter
250 g (8 oz) icing
 sugar
TO DECORATE:
wafers
wafer-thin chocolate
 mints

Line and grease an 18 x 28 cm (7 x 11 inch) Swiss roll tin, leaving 2.5 cm (1 inch) paper above the sides.

Blend the cocoa with the water; cool slightly. Cream the fat and sugar until light and fluffy; beat in the cocoa.

Beat in the eggs one at a time, adding a tablespoon of the flour with the last two. Fold in the remaining flour and turn into the prepared tin. Bake in a preheated moderately hot oven, 190°C (375°F), Gas Mark 5, for 25 to 30 minutes. Turn onto a wire rack to cool.

Make the icing as for Devil's Food Cake (page 18).

Cut a 3.5 cm (1½ inch) strip from one end of the cake and cut into 4 squares. Cut the remaining cake in half and sandwich together with icing. Cover the top and sides of the cake with icing, smooth, then mark lines for bricks. Cover the squares with the remaining icing and place on the corners for turrets.

Cut the wafers to make windows and a door and place in position. Cut the mints into small squares and place between the turrets for battlements. Finish with flags at each corner and toy soldiers.
Makes one castle cake

21st Birthday Cake

325 g (11 oz) plain
  flour
2 teaspoons ground
  mixed spice
½ teaspoon grated
  nutmeg
300 g (10 oz) butter
  or margarine
300 g (10 oz) soft
  brown sugar
grated rind of
  1 lemon
2 tablespoons black
  treacle
6 eggs
75 g (3 oz) ground
  almonds
500 g (1 lb) currants
325 g (11 oz)
  sultanas
175 g (6 oz) raisins
125 g (4 oz) glacé
  cherries, quartered
125 g (4 oz)
  chopped mixed
  peel
125 g (4 oz) split
  almonds, chopped
ALMOND PASTE:
525 g (1¼ lb)
  ground almonds
300 g (10 oz) caster
  sugar
300 g (10 oz) icing
  sugar
2 eggs
2 teaspoons lemon
  juice
½ teaspoon almond
  essence
4 tablespoons
  warmed, sieved
  apricot jam

Prepare a deep 23 cm (9 inch) square cake tin as for Boiled Fruit Cake (page 17). Make, bake and store the cake as for Dundee Cake (page 16), adding the treacle with the fat and sugar and the chopped and ground almonds with the fruit.

Make the almond paste and cover the cake as for Christmas Cake (page 84).

Make the royal icing as for Christmas Cake. Put half the icing on top of the cake, keeping the rest covered with a damp cloth. Spread the icing over the top of the cake with a palette knife. Pull an icing ruler over the icing to make a smooth flat surface. Remove any excess icing and leave for 24 hours.

Spread two-thirds of the remaining icing around the sides of the cake, and smooth with a palette knife. Remove surplus icing from the bottom and top edges and leave to set for 24 hours.

Place the remaining icing in a piping bag fitted with a plain writing nozzle and decorate the cake with a lattice pattern (as shown). Pipe lines at 5 mm (¼ inch) intervals diagonally across the corners, then pipe lines across these at right angles. When dry, pipe lines at right angles on top of these, but slightly longer to make a neat finish.

To form the lattice at the bottom of the cake, pipe lines from the board about 1 cm (½ inch) away from the cake diagonally 1 cm (½ inch) up the cake. Repeat the lines at 1 cm (½ inch) intervals all round the cake, then pipe a second set of lines diagonally opposite. When dry pipe another line on top. Using a small shell pipe, pipe a border of shells along the edge of the lattice.

ROYAL ICING:
5 egg whites
1.25 kg (2½ lb)
  icing sugar
2 teaspoons lemon
  juice
3 teaspoons glycerine
few drops of food
  colouring

Colour a little of the icing, put into a small icing bag fitted with a writing nozzle and pipe 21 on top of the cake. Decorate the sides with sugar roses, if liked.

Makes one 25 cm (10 inch) cake

Simnel Cake

200 g (7 oz) plain
flour
2 teaspoons ground
mixed spice
175 g (6 oz) butter
or margarine
175 g (6 oz) soft
brown sugar
grated rind of
1 orange
4 eggs
175 g (6 oz) currants
175 g (6 oz)
sultanas
175 g (6 oz) raisins
75 g (3 oz) glacé
cherries, quartered
50 g (2 oz) chopped
mixed peel
ALMOND PASTE:
350 g (12 oz)
ground almonds
175 g (6 oz) icing
sugar
175 g (6 oz) caster
sugar
1 large egg
4 drops of almond
essence
2 teaspoons lemon
juice
1 tablespoon
warmed, sieved
apricot jam

Prepare a 19 cm (7½ inch) cake tin as for Boiled Fruit Cake (page 17). Make the cake as for Dundee Cake (page 16). Make the almond paste as for Christmas Cake (page 84) and roll out one quarter into a 19 cm (7½ inch) circle.

Place half the cake mixture in the prepared tin, lay the circle of almond paste on top and press down lightly. Place the remaining cake mixture on top and smooth the surface.

Bake in a preheated moderate oven, 160°C (325°F), Gas Mark 3, for 1 hour, then lower the temperature to 150°C (300°F), Gas Mark 2 and bake for a further 2½ hours or until a skewer inserted into the centre comes out clean. Leave in the tin for 5 minutes then turn onto a wire rack to cool.

Roll one third of the remaining almond paste into a circle to fit the top of the cake. Brush the cake with apricot jam and press the paste into place. Shape the remaining paste into small balls and arrange around the top of the cake. Place under a hot grill to brown the balls. Tie a yellow ribbon round the cake and decorate as liked, with sweet eggs, etc.
Makes one 19 cm (7½ inch) cake

Easter Truffles

175 g (6 oz) plain
chocolate
1 egg yolk
25 g (1 oz) butter
1 teaspoon coffee
essence
1 tablespoon cocoa

Melt the chocolate in a bowl over a pan of hot water. Add the egg yolk, butter and coffee essence and leave in a cool place for 30 to 40 minutes until set.

Mould into small egg shapes with the fingers and roll in the cocoa to coat evenly.
Makes 20

INDEX

Acknowledgments

Photography by Paul Williams
Food prepared by Carole Handslip
Designed by Astrid Publishing Consultants Ltd